THE

ART OF

PITCHING

THE
ART OF
PITCHING

by TOM SEAVER
with Lee Lowenfish

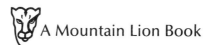

A Mountain Lion Book

Published by
HEARST BOOKS   New York

Library of Congress Catalog Card Number: 83-83031

ISBN: 0-688-13226-X

Printed in the United States of America

1 2 3 4 5 6 7 8 9 10

For Sarah and Anne—for all the joy you have given me

GTS

To the memory of my mother and father

LEL

ACKNOWLEDGMENTS

Special thanks go to the following individuals who shared research materials: Tony Connor, Tom Felle, Stephen E. Gould, Dr. Stan Grosshandler, Jack Lang, Ed Linn, Susan B. Lowe, Larry Mayol, John Monteleone, Bob Morgens, Jeff Neuman, Pete Palmer, Dan Rosen, Sheldon Sunness, Judythe Wilbur, and Charles Woolston. Jay Horwitz and Lorraine Doran Hamilton of the New York Mets public relations staff provided swift and helpful answers to our queries and requests for assistance. Joan Nagy and Ian Gonzalez at William Morrow gave us extremely helpful editorial advice and their enthusiasm was an added bonus. New York Met trainer Larry Mayol gave us the benefit of his close reading of Chapters 2 and 8.

Lee Lowenfish wishes to express thanks to his nephew, Eric Norton, for explaining some of the mysteries of computer programs. Thanks, too, to Fred Herschkowitz who helped him become a part of this project. As always, his wife, Greta Minsky, contributed her keen editorial advice and her unflagging sympathy when this project entered the late innings and her husband could be heard muttering constantly, "I want that complete game!"

CONTENTS

THE
ART OF
PITCHING

1

THE CHALLENGE OF PITCHING

It is a steamy summer afternoon in St. Louis, Missouri, and you are pitching in a close game against the Cardinals. You have been in command of your pitches all day and are nursing a small lead. But as the game enters the late innings, you realize that your stuff isn't as effective as it had been. Your fastball's slowed down, and your slider's not breaking as sharply as it should.

The oppressive heat brings the temperature on the artificial surface at Busch Memorial Stadium to a sizzling 140 degrees, to say nothing of the humidity. An ordinary mortal might be forgiven for daydreaming about an afternoon at the beach, or anticipating the ice-cold drink that awaits him in the clubhouse.

But a professional pitcher can't indulge in such fantasies. Hot or cold, you have a game to play, and you must put everything else out of your mind, whether it's a quarrel with your wife, the shortstop's glaring error on the last play, your kid's case of the chicken pox, or an umpire's missed call. You have a job to do that requires 100 percent of your mental energy and 100 percent of your physical energy. You must plan ahead. Not only do you have the next batter to set up, but you must also try to avoid having a runner in scoring position when that hot hitter who's been hitting .380 for the past two weeks comes up to the plate. You must be able to plan strategies far in advance while concentrating on each and every pitch. Pitching is not a job for the physically timid or the mentally lazy.

I remember a game early in my major-league career when I went head to head with the great Bob Gibson of St. Louis, a pitcher destined for the Hall of Fame. The heat was almost unbearable and there may have been extra medical personnel on hand inside the stadium in the event fans succumbed to heat prostration. I changed my undershirt after every inning of work to keep the perspiration from collecting against my body.

As uncomfortable as the evening felt, I vowed to maintain total concentration on the task at hand. My teammates had given me an early lead over Gibson who, after a shaky start, had found his normal groove. I sensed that the two-run lead I still held in the bottom of the seventh inning was all that I would have to work with. A professional pitcher's greatest test is to hold on to a lead that his teammates have given him.

Suddenly, I found myself in a jam in the seventh with no outs and runners on second and third. The Cardinals' excellent table setters, Lou Brock and Curt Flood, the first two men in the batting order, had singled and doubled, respectively. The tying runs were on and the meat of the order was coming up.

As the left-handed slugger Roger Maris stepped in, I evaluated the situation. Brock and Flood hit good pitches, I told myself, so give them credit but don't get down on yourself. "If Brock scores, you will still have a one-run lead," I thought. "Don't get greedy. Just make sure that Maris doesn't get a pitch that will score Flood or bring him to third with less than two out." I bore down on Maris and got him to hit a short fly ball that did not advance the runners. With the big advantage of having earned the first out, I could work to cleanup hitter Orlando Cepeda, and the left-handed-hitting catcher Tim McCarver, knowing that if I made good pitches, only one run could score on an out.

The story of this game in St. Louis's draining heat had a happy ending for me. One run did score, but I protected our one-run lead for the rest of the game. Other stories of close games don't end so happily for me, but they still reveal the essence of pitching's challenge, the constant one-on-one confrontation between pitcher and hitter. Such bracing competition is the lifeblood of our craft. All real pitchers thrive on it, live for it.

On another hot summer day, this time in Chicago in 1969, I faced a similar challenge. It was my first start after having nearly hurled a perfect game against the Cubs in New York. It was the bottom of the sixth in a scoreless pitchers' duel against

Bill Hands. The Cubs had Glenn Beckert on second with two out and their left-handed-hitting outfielder, Billy Williams, at the plate. Billy was one of those great hitters who could go to any field. In a key situation, I often tried to make Billy pull the ball; it was about the only way to try to defuse him. He kept spoiling many good pitches, and it was a long at-bat. Finally, I threw him yet another high, inside pitch, trying to make him pull, but he singled past shortstop for the only RBI in the game. I lost the battle and the game that day, but in my seventeen-year major-league career, I have won a good share of the battles.

A successful starting pitcher, who more often than not completes his nine-inning assignments, will throw between 110 and 130 pitches in a given game. Every few seconds he has to decide what kind of pitch to throw. If he is thinking ahead, he will select pitches in sequence—for instance, throwing a sinking fastball in spot A in order to get the batter out with a slider in spot B. Since the ball is released in less than a second and often, alas, comes back the other way far more quickly, there is some fast thinking required.

According to the rules, a baseball must weigh between five and five and one-quarter ounces and have a circumference of between nine and nine and one-quarter inches. There are 108 tight stitches on the seam of each ball. How you handle the baseball determines your livelihood, and you should develop the feel for it that an artist has for his paintbrush.

Any pitcher interested in accepting the challenges of the craft must understand that every baseball pitch possesses three physical attributes: velocity (speed), movement (liveliness), and location (control). A major-league pitcher cannot survive on velocity alone. The pages of baseball history are littered with footnotes about flame-throwers who never learned to control the ball. But a pitcher who can make his ball move and control its destination has the potential to master the art of pitching; however, such mastery comes only through infinite patience and constant practice.

Once you have a feel for the ball and understand the three attributes of baseball pitches, you should acknowledge a few basic truths about the game and learn to rely on these truths as you plan your strategy.

Only three or four outs directly affect the outcome of any given game. Stated another way, a game may ride on just three or four pitches that the pitcher must choose carefully and throw with accuracy. No matter how lopsided the final score, you can usually pinpoint the moment that a key out was made or not made and a vital pitch was thrown well or misthrown.

One of the greatest challenges of pitching is to recognize these critical situations and to rise to the occasion with consistency and a competitive spirit. You can train yourself to identify the outs that you *must* get, and within the bounds of sportsmanship, to go about getting them. You must be like a prizefighter going after his opponent. Once you have him cornered or hurt, you must keep the pressure on. Make the batter try to go after the pitch you throw, not wait for the pitch he wants.

Get ahead on the count is another pitching maxim. The art of pitching is complex but counting balls and strikes is simple. The pitcher has a built-in edge because he can throw one more ball than the batter can have strikes. If you go 0–1 on a batter and even better 0–2, you have put the hitter at a distinct disadvantage. You have made him a defensive hitter. But if you fall behind 1–0, you approach the real danger zone for a pitcher of 2–0 and 3–1 counts.

Statistical studies, which baseball teams employ more and more often these days, graphically demonstrate the importance of getting ahead on the count. Pete Palmer, a computer programmer at the Sports Information Center in Boston, Massachusetts, studied thousands of pitching counts during World Series and League Championship Series games in the 1970's. He discovered that batters with an 0–2 count hit collectively for only a .191 average, whereas hitters with a 3–1 advantage on the count tattooed pitchers for a .324 average. He found that eighth-position hitters with a 1–0 count hit for better averages than cleanup (fourth-place) sluggers behind 0 and 1 in the count.

Palmer also learned that more than 80 percent of bases on balls occur when the first pitch is a ball. Hitters ahead 1–0 on the count are more than twice as likely to drive in or score runs (or both) than hitters whom the pitchers get ahead of. Perhaps most striking was Palmer's discovery that in 76 percent of cases in which a walk was granted to open an inning the base runner eventually scored.

I cannot stress too much how important it is for a pitcher to avoid walks. Even if you manage to keep the runner from scoring, you have unnecessarily made yourself work harder. You have given the batter a free ticket, something he has not earned by his own effort. There are times when advanced baseball strategy dictates an intentional walk to a powerhouse hitter whom you'd rather see on first base than threatening you at the plate. But, in general, common sense and statistics concur: *Get ahead on the count.*

Another maxim is: *Get the first out of an inning.* The successful pitcher will be the one who gets the first out of an inning most of the time. If you get the first out, your defense may be able to end the inning with a double play. (They don't call the dp "a pitcher's best friend" for nothing!) Getting the first out also usually eliminates the possibility of a surprise bunt. In general, it shows your opponent that you are in command from the start.

The successful pitcher will have learned as second nature two more fundamental truths about containing hitters.

(1) *Don't let the batter make contact with the meat of the bat.* The Baseball Rule Book says that a bat can be no more than forty-two inches long or two and three-quarter inches thick at the point of its greatest circumference. A pitcher can take solace in knowing that only about eight inches on the bat can really do him harm. The essence of good pitching is to move the ball around the plate so deviously that the batter rarely makes contact with those eight inches of the bat.

(2) *Don't let the batter claim both sides of the plate.* The rule book decrees that home plate be seventeen inches wide. The strike zone is defined as "that space over home plate between

A baseball bat can be as long as forty-two inches (the average is between thirty-four and a half and thirty-five inches) but the only place on the bat that can do a pitcher real harm is in the sweet middle portion, which is about eight inches long. Good pitching is premised on moving the baseball away from the danger black spot into the gray zones on the handle or the end of the bat.

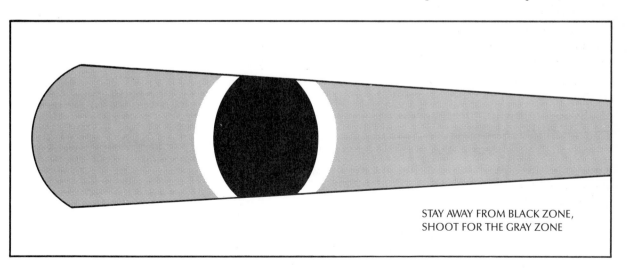

STAY AWAY FROM BLACK ZONE,
SHOOT FOR THE GRAY ZONE

the batter's armpits and the top of his knees when he assumes his natural stance," as determined by the plate umpire. The batter has a rightful claim to the middle of the plate, but a good pitcher makes his living on the corners and, through deception, off the corners of the plate. If you feel that the batter is leaning over the plate and trying to claim all of it, you must jam him from time to time, throwing hard stuff inside. By "inside," I mean the area from the edge of the inside corner of the plate toward the batter's midsection. We call that a batter's "kitchen." A good pitcher wants to get into the hitter's kitchen and break some of his dishes.

Your control over the velocity, movement, and location of your pitches can vary greatly from outing to outing, so you must be sufficiently objective to detect and, if necessary, compensate for these differences every time you go to work. Close communication with your catcher is a necessity in this regard. Very often, after a pitcher completes his follow-through, he is off-balance and cannot accurately observe the response of the batter to the ball in the hitting zone. An alert catcher can provide valuable assistance in the important task of monitoring the batters' reactions to your pitches.

For instance, is the batter making contact behind, even with, or in front of the plate? If he is behind and thus late with his swing, you know that your fastball has good velocity that day. If he is making contact even with the plate, it is a standoff between you and the batter. If the hitter is reaching the ball in front of the plate, then he is ahead of you and you must be ready to adjust your pitch selection and location, and maybe prepare to fool him with a change-up.

You must observe where on the bat the hitter is connecting with the ball. Are you sawing him off on the handle or forcing him to make contact only with the end of the bat? If you and your catcher detect this happening, then it is safe to conclude that your ball is moving properly.

You must also closely watch the movement of the batter's body into the ball. Is he lowering his front shoulder? This is usually the sign of a fleet, ground-ball singles hitter, and you might decide to pitch him up and in. Is he keeping his hands behind him on the bat, even while he strides forward with his front foot? This is usually the sign of a great hitter, who can commit part of his body to a pitch while maintaining sufficient control and arm strength to do you damage at the last split-second. Willie Mays and Roberto Clemente had this superior ability to wait on a pitch with their arms back, even as they stepped forward. There was no set way to pitch to them except to vary your pitch selection while remaining alert to signs of particular strengths, weaknesses, or preferences that they exhibited in any given at-bat.

Having stated these general truths, let me emphasize that one of the greatest challenges of pitching is adjusting the basic theory to the specific reality of the kind of stuff you have or may not have on a given day on the mound.

Pitching can be a very humbling profession, and while we strive for perfection, we never fully attain it. Even in a shutout a pitcher invariably makes five or seven mistakes, although in that particular game the batters did not take advantage of them. A wise pitcher is one who knows he made a mistake even when he got away with it. Learn to recognize your mistakes and discipline yourself to avoid them. For instance, you have a hitter in a hole on an 0–2 count. You want to throw a fastball out of the strike zone, but you throw it in the strike zone and get a strikeout. Against a better hitter, that strikeout pitch might have been tagged for a hit when you should have had the batter at your mercy.

Sooner or later, sloppiness when you are ahead in the count will catch up with you. I have learned from hard experience that *the higher up you go on the ladder of pro baseball, the more batters will take advantage of your mistakes.* Nobody is perfect and we all will make mistakes on the mound. But our goal must be not to make the same ones over and over again. Know yourself and what your pitches are intended to accomplish. Learn to avoid those mistakes that the major-league batter will take advantage of as much as 90 percent of the time.

Just as you need to recognize your mistakes, you must also know when you have thrown a good pitch even if it was safely hit. Batters will, at times, send your best offering out of the ball park. You can't mope about it, but must accept it as a fact of baseball life. Remember that baseball gods are inscrutable deities, not easily fathomed but mercilessly regular in their ways. The very best teams will lose at least 62 games in a 162-game season, and the very best pitchers will be hit safely against at least a few times a game.

Never underestimate the ability of a hitter. While the law of averages always favors a pitcher, good hitters will sometimes hit good pitches. It's a fact of baseball life.

I recall one day in Pittsburgh when I had one of my greatest nemeses, Willie Stargell, deep in a hole with an 0–2 count. Knowing that Willie feasted on fastballs, I threw him a change-up exactly where I wanted: low and away, outside the strike zone by at least four inches. Willie was caught off-stride and swung one-handed off his front foot, as I intended. He lofted a fly ball to center field and with two out, I started walking toward the visitors' dugout near third base. When I looked around, however, I saw our center fielder racing to the wall in vain pursuit of a home run that landed more than four hundred feet away in dead center. I almost collided with Willie near the third-base line as he was completing his home-run trot. As I walked back to the mound, he needled me good-naturedly, "Where are you goin', man?"

On other days, that pitch might have gotten Willie out, but he beat me that day. The point is to accept the momentary setback, knowing that a good hitter will occasionally crush your best offering, and vow to get him the next time.

On the other hand, if you don't know the difference between good hitting and bad pitching, you are heading for stormy waters. We have all seen pitchers with the greatest stuff in the world who never seem to rise above the mediocrity of a .500 record. They pitch, as the phrase goes, "just well enough to lose." They lack the ability to distinguish between their mistakes and good pitches well hit. They overestimate how well they are pitching on a given day, and when they are tagged, they lose confidence. Instead of battling back with their best stuff, they become defensive and hesitant on the mound.

There is nothing worse than throwing *any* pitch with less than 100 percent commitment. Batters see everything a pitcher does on the mound from a distance of sixty feet, six inches. They recognize hesitation and know that a halfhearted pitch is coming. Halfhearted pitches invariably are mistake pitches, and before long, the hesitant hurler will be looking for another occupation.

Even a talented, dedicated pitcher who learns from his mistakes and tries to correct them will inevitably have to endure a slump. Batting slumps are a topic of regular discussion among the press and the fans, but you hear very little about pitching slumps. They happen all the time, and another challenge of pitching is to accept them and battle your way through them. One game or one inning will not get you into a slump, and one game or one inning will not get you out of a slump. But if you constantly monitor your performance, pitch by pitch, you can limit the severity of a slump to a game or two.

When in a slump, watching films of your good outings can help (seeing bad outings again may only depress you but can be beneficial on a comparison basis). Analyzing your motion in a mirror may also help. I was impressed during my two trips to Japan in the 1970's that all the professional Japanese baseball teams had full-length mirrors in their clubhouses. Pitchers and hitters alike regularly practice their motions in front of these mirrors. Clad only in jogging shorts and tennis shoes, the players get a daily education in how all the parts of the body function together. American clubs would do well to install mirrors and encourage their use.

In trying to conquer a pitching slump, don't panic and overhaul your mechanics. The problem is almost always minor and needs only a small adjustment. When I pitched for the Cincinnati Reds, my teammate Tom Hume was having a hard time. He told me, "I feel like I'm falling back on the mound. . . . I can't get the ball down." I observed Tommy's motion, placed my hands on his shoulders, and brought them slightly forward. After this minor adjustment, Tommy went on to a highly successful season. Despite battles with injury, he has established himself as a premier National League short-relief specialist.

When I'm suffering through a slump, I remind myself of a basic rule of pitching: *Throw strikes, and throw low strikes.* By low strikes I mean pitches that are no more than six inches above the knee. Throwing *low* strikes aids the pitcher because the batter sees less of the ball when it is thrown low. He is likely to hit it on the ground and with less authority, and if he does connect, it won't be as damaging. A batter sees the entire back half of the baseball when it is thrown high.

Remind yourself, too, that the pitcher has the advantage. He gets a batter out with three strikes while the batter needs four balls to walk. If you can get ahead of him on the count, you have even more of an edge. Remember how poorly batters hit when behind in the count.

As I said at the outset, pitching is not a career for the mentally lazy or the physically timid. But if you have the toughness, the desire, and the basic raw talent, there is no greater joy than being a consistent, durable, winning pitcher, working his 250-plus innings and 35-plus starts season after season. I have sometimes envied the regular player who gets to perform this great game of baseball at least 162 meaningful times a year. But the nonpitcher does not get to enjoy that peak of satisfaction that a starting pitcher experiences if he is working every fourth or fifth day.

Pitching is an acquired art, a fact that I can attest to in my own career. I never enjoyed the luxury (or perhaps the trap) of high school success. I did not make my high school varsity team in Fresno, California, until my senior year, and then I barely posted a .500 record. I was a five-foot nine-inch, 165-pound junkball pitcher who upon graduation was unsigned by any major-league organization and was uncertain about his future.

I went into a Marine Corps reserve program. Eighteen months later, I had grown four inches, added thirty-five pounds, and discovered that I now possessed a live fastball. After a year in junior college, I obtained an athletic scholarship to the University of Southern California. I came under the tutelage of Rod Dedeaux, USC's legendary baseball coach who has produced such major-league pitchers as Steve Busby, Bill Lee, and Pete Redfern, and such nonpitching stars as Ron Fairly, Rich Dauer, Steve Kemp, and Roy Smalley.

Rod Dedeaux helped me make the transition from a "thrower" to a pitcher who understood how to set up hitters and change speeds on his pitches. Signed by the New York Mets in 1966, I spent one year in the minor leagues for the Mets' Triple A Jacksonville, Florida, farm team, where I compiled only a .500 record. I arrived in the major leagues to stay in 1967.

What follows in *The Art of Pitching* is no academic exercise. With the help of some of my most talented colleagues, I will share with you my understanding of what it means to put on your spikes, go out to the mound, and contend with formidable major-league hitters.

2 THE ABSOLUTES OF PITCHING PREPARATION

OFF-SEASON PREPARATION

A well-executed pitch is one of the most graphic images in sports. The rhythm of a body in harmony is a joy to see. But it is even more rewarding to be able to perform such artistry.

Jim Palmer has said that when he is pitching well, he can almost see where the ball will go before he has thrown it. At the top of his game, Sandy Koufax talked about the baseball as an extension of his body. On good days, I feel that I have absolute control of the ball and can direct my pitches "on the black," the edges of the plate where batters can do no harm.

Good pitching is not achieved by magic. It comes from hard work and an understanding of what the body can and cannot do. Pitching requires the participation and coordination of all the muscles of the body, especially the shoulder muscles and the large muscles of the lower body: the calves, thighs, back, and buttocks. People often talk with awe about a pitcher's great arm, but the successful, durable pitcher must keep his entire body finely conditioned.

The recent national concern for physical fitness is also reflected in the major leagues. All year round, most modern ballplayers exercise to maintain their strength and flexibility. And that is the objective of the following exercises—strength and flexibility. Playing the game of baseball does not require weightlifters' muscles; they probably do more harm than good.

But you do need to prepare your body to throw and hit the baseball. The exercises I perform, and those described here, are specifically designed to help you withstand the strains of the long baseball season.

I remember walking into my first Mets' spring-training club-house carrying the ten-pound dumbbell I had used at the University of Southern California. "Whaddaya got there, Atlas?" snickered some of the older veterans who had rarely approached the playing of baseball in a scientific way. In the old days, spring training often became a contest of seeing who could lose the most winter weight. In today's fitness-conscious sports world, the value of maintaining proper muscle tone all year round is happily stressed. It makes far greater sense to use the preseason to fine-tune your muscles into playing shape than to spend that valuable time removing excess fat.

Keeping the Arm and Shoulder Fit

In my eighteen years of pitching, the emphasis on conditioning, weight training, and flexibility is one of the most dramatic changes I've seen.

I will always be grateful to Jerry Merz, a friend and a pitcher at the University of Southern California, who first impressed upon me the importance of working with small weights. The numerous arm and shoulder muscles involved in the throwing of a baseball can be strengthened by weight exercises. Larry Mayol, my trainer on the Mets, declares flatly, "I can get any pitcher prepared for the game of baseball by working him with weights of ten pounds or less and varying the repetitions." Larry and I firmly believe that these small-weight exercises can help you develop vital strength and flexibility in the shoulder, wrist, and elbow of both your throwing and your nonthrowing arms.

The shoulder is one of the body's most complicated mechanisms. As many as fifty arm and shoulder muscles are involved in throwing a baseball. The most important of these constitute the rotator cuff, a series of four muscles that hold the upper-arm bone (the humerus) to the roof of the shoulder (the glenoid labrum). The four muscles of the rotator cuff are the supraspinatus, the infraspinatus, the teres minor, and the subscapularis. The supraspinatus muscle is especially important in pitching because during the follow-through it keeps the shoulder fixed to the head of the humerus. Like all voluntary muscles in the body, those of the rotator cuff operate in pairs, one contracting while the other relaxes.

Maintaining a healthy rotator cuff will enable you to establish and sustain the full range of motion needed for successful pitching. Its efficiency is central to your pitching longevity. A dreaded tear or rupture can shorten or end your career. It will certainly make you a less effective pitcher.

Regular workouts with weights of three to ten pounds can help keep you from unwelcome dates with medical dictionaries and physicians. These weights are not very expensive. If you are a high school, college, or semipro player with professional ambitions and you do not have access to the sophisticated training devices and professional trainer assistance available in organized pro baseball, weight work on your own can keep you fit throughout the calendar.

I perform the exercises demonstrated on these pages by Larry Mayol three times a week during the off-season. Before I begin, I always make sure that I am warmed up and have broken a sweat. Simple calisthenics, running, or swinging a bat will serve this purpose.

There are as many as fifty muscles in the shoulder, but the ones most vital to pitching and throwing are the four muscles of the rotator cuff. Pictured here are the supraspinatus, the infraspinatus, and the teres minor. Resting beneath these muscles, and therefore not visible in the drawing, is the subscapularis.

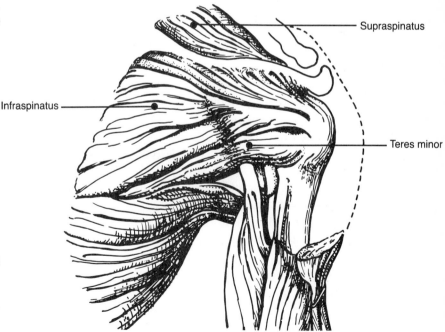

Supraspinatus

Infraspinatus

Teres minor

ROTATOR CUFF MUSCLES

The warm-up does two things: It stimulates the blood flow in your cardiovascular system to the area of the arm and shoulder that you are planning to exercise. It also makes sure that the muscles are loosened and not cold, thereby preventing dangerous pulls.

Once warmed up, you can start these small-weight exercises, using weights between three and five pounds. It is important to do the exercises with the proper form and the proper mechanics. It is better to complete three sets of five repetitions with pauses of a minute between each set than to jerk your way through two sets of ten repetitions using momentum rather than steady effort to strengthen your muscles. A goal of three sets of ten repetitions for each exercise is reasonable for an aspiring pitcher, but don't expect to fulfill it immediately. These exercises promote equal strength in the upper arm and shoulder muscles throughout the full range of motion. Remember that all your muscles are paired. For every concentric contraction of your biceps, for example, there is an eccentric contraction of your triceps. All these exercises duplicate the movements required in pitching. They will help to increase flexibility as well as strengthen your arm and shoulder, not only on your pitching side but also for your gloved arm and shoulder.

Everyone's strength potential is different. Exercises with weights should be noncompetitive. If you find that working out is more enjoyable with a teammate, good. But don't get into a contest with him. The objective is not to be able to do more than your friend, but only enough to increase *your* strength.

The objective of small-weight work is worth repeating: *to obtain equal strength throughout the entire range of motion of the shoulder muscles.* You achieve this by slowly lifting the weights against the force of gravity. If you use force or momentum to carry you through these exercises, you are only fooling yourself. Larry Mayol has a vivid way of describing what happens when you improperly jerk your way through these drills. "It's like adding ten feet of link to a strong chain," he says. "If you haven't strengthened that new linkage, you have weakened the entire chain."

The correct way to exercise is to ease into each exercise slowly, count to five or six, ease out, relax for a few seconds, and then repeat the exercise. Each individual will have his own starting point and endurance level. These will increase as the drills are faithfully performed.

There should be no pain or discomfort in these exercises. Do them to the point of fatigue, rest, and start again. If there is pain or soreness, it won't be eased with continued aggravation. Give the muscles a rest of a week or ten days and then resume the exercises. If there is still soreness, consult a physician.

Most often when there is damage to the rotator cuff, the supraspinatus muscle registers some discomfort. The isolation of this key muscle is a good way to test its strength. Exercise 3 is designed to strengthen the supraspinatus.

Some of the weight exercises are performed lying on your side on a trainer's table. If you are doing these exercises without professional assistance, make sure that you have stabilized your elbow and locked your wrist. Notice the firmness of Larry's position on the table in Exercise 4 as he prepares to strengthen his rotators in one or two sets of ten repetitions.

Remember, if at first you can only do one set with five or six repetitions, don't be discouraged. Accept that as your starting point and work toward a goal of increased repetitions. But do the work honestly. Don't cheat yourself.

Exercise 5 is done lying face up on a table. If you perform this exercise unassisted, be certain to keep your elbow stabilized.

Exercises 6 and 7 are performed lying face down on a table. Three sets of ten repetitions is an optimum goal. These exercises will increase both your forearm and shoulder strength.

I perform these exercises for approximately twenty-five minutes three times a week during the off-season. (The days off allow your muscles to recover and your energy supply to be replenished.) Since I have the service of an expert trainer like Larry Mayol available during the season, I confine my small-weight work to the off-season. For the amateur pitcher who lacks access to a trainer and will therefore be unable to do the exercises described in Chapter 8, I strongly recommend using these weights to maintain fitness throughout your entire season but on a limited basis.

Small-weight work executed properly reproduces all the motions of pitching, from windup to cocking to acceleration and follow-through. But they are certainly not the only exercises that will ensure pitching fitness. Ferguson Jenkins realized that his forearm needed strengthening if he was to become a successful and durable pitcher. On the advice of Gene Dziadura, the scout who signed him, Ferguson worked out in the off-season with a five-pound sledgehammer that helped him build up his

Exercise 1. To exercise the forward bending of the shoulder (*flexion*), start with the weights in front of you and raise them until they are parallel to the floor. Turn the weights upright and raise them to the ceiling. Pause at the top and then reverse the sequence and return to the starting position.

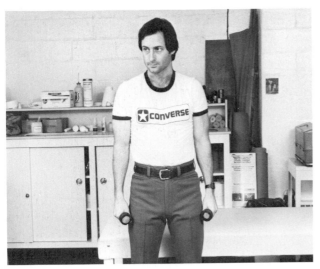

Exercise 2. To exercise the shoulder muscles that pull the arm away from the midline of the body (*abduction*), start with the weights at your side. Bring them to an outstretched position and rotate your arms, the palms face upward. Raise the arms to the ceiling, pause, and reverse the sequence to return to the starting position.

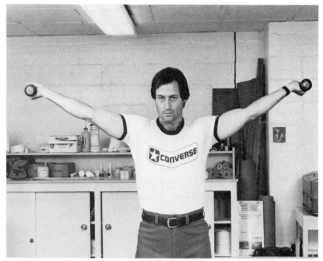

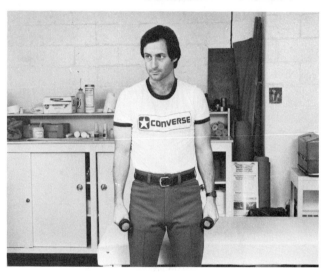

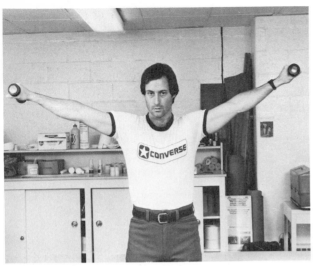

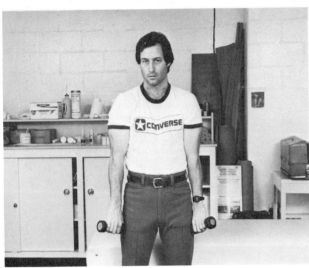

Exercise 3. This is an important exercise for isolating the supraspinatus muscle. Start with the arms in an outstretched position. Then rotate them forward about thirty degrees with the thumbs pointing straight down. Maintaining the thirty-degree position, slowly lower your arms to your sides and then return to the starting position.

Exercise 4. To build up the external rotators in your shoulder, lie on your left side on a table with your left elbow stabilized beneath you. Hold the weight close to your waist with your right wrist locked, establishing an *L* between your upper arm and your forearm. Ease the weight up toward the ceiling, pause, and then return to the starting position.

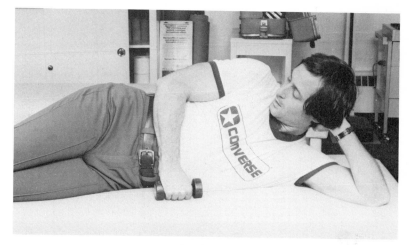

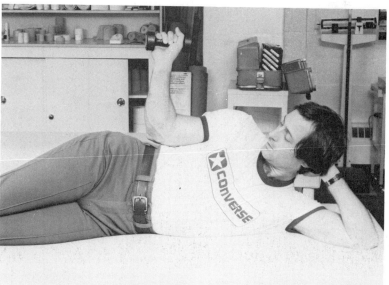

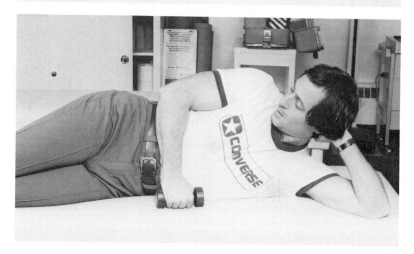

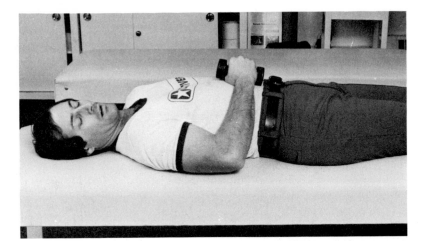

Exercise 5. To build up the internal rotators in your shoulder, lie on your back with the weight in your right hand and your elbow as close to the table as possible. Bring the weight outward, pause, and return it to the starting position.

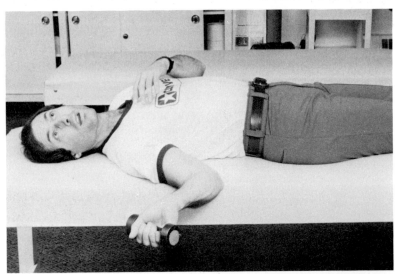

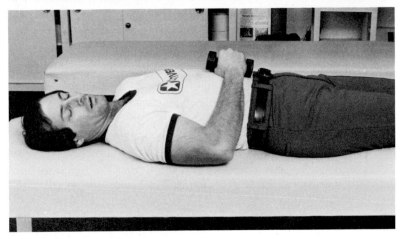

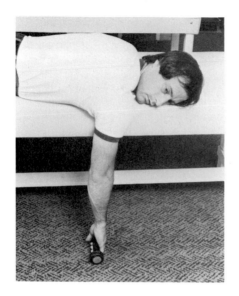

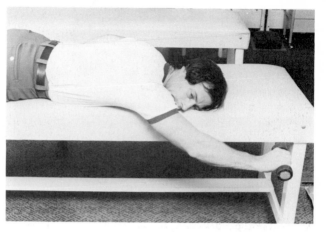

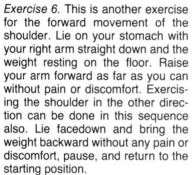

Exercise 6. This is another exercise for the forward movement of the shoulder. Lie on your stomach with your right arm straight down and the weight resting on the floor. Raise your arm forward as far as you can without pain or discomfort. Exercising the shoulder in the other direction can be done in this sequence also. Lie facedown and bring the weight backward without any pain or discomfort, pause, and return to the starting position.

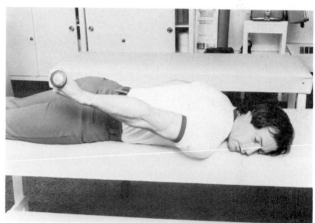

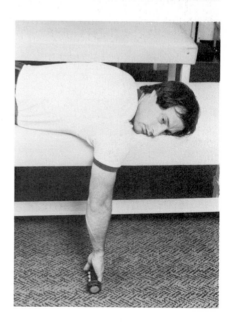

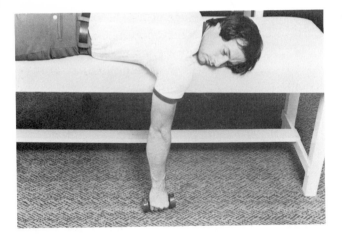

Exercise 7. The final exercise in this sequence strengthens the shoulder muscles that draw the arm to the midline of the body (*adduction*). Lie on your stomach with your arm straight down and the weight resting on the floor. Bring the weight out parallel to the floor, pause, and return to the starting position.

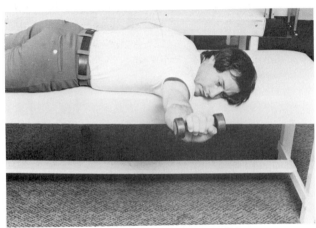

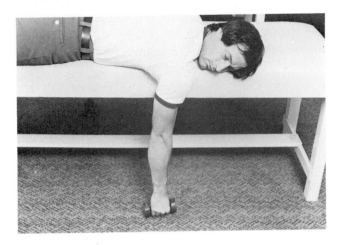

forearm and wrist. Under the tutelage of weight-training coach Gus Hoefling, Steve Carlton has achieved awesome strength in his arms and body by performing an elaborate series of martial arts exercises and weight training. Exercising his left arm by moving it through a bucket of rice is part of Steve's training program; other pitchers have started to try this, too.

But, as I will say many times in this book, do not imitate me, Steve Carlton, Nolan Ryan, or any of your heroes as you begin to study the art of pitching. We are all individuals with unique abilities, limitations, and endurance levels. Find out what kind of program will achieve the desired end of strength and flexibility for your own particular physique and needs. Just make sure you understand why it is important that you not overdo weight work—and stick to the small weights under ten pounds. Pitching fitness is far different from weightlifting prowess. Teenagers especially should be wary of body-building programs that can retard the normal growth of their bone structures.

Keeping the Legs Fit

A wise man once said about aging baseball players that "the legs are the first to go." It's especially true for pitchers, who must drive off the mound on each and every pitch.

During the off-season, I don't engage in as elaborate a program of leg strengthening and flexibility as I use for the arm and shoulder. Part of the reason is that my lower body is heavily muscled. To maintain the natural strength in these muscles, I perform squats in a series of ten repetitions using hundred-pound weights on my shoulders. This complements my thrice-weekly winter small-weight work.

During the season, between starts, I do standing straight-leg lifts and bent-leg lifts, a series of ten repetitions for each leg. I step up on a chair with my toe turned in and then out, and stretch and strengthen my thigh muscles by trying to lift myself up. I also work with a weighted leg boot of approximately fifteen to twenty pounds. Lying on an incline, I lift the boot up and down, slowly and regularly as in all the weight work, in a series of fifteen to twenty repetitions.

My legs are strong enough not to require heavier weights, but every pitcher has his own preference. Nolan Ryan, an awesome physical specimen, feels comfortable exercising with leg boots carrying as much as one hundred pounds. You cannot argue with his success, but don't imitate him. In consultation with a trainer and a coach, and by your own self-assessment, find a program that best prepares your legs to suit your own needs.

The primary exercise is running. Throughout his great career, Jim Palmer has run five miles the day after the season ended to remind himself that his heartbeat and stamina must be maintained vigilantly and that he must continue regular running in the off-season. I often play squash during the off-season to keep myself running, but as the season nears and once it is in swing, there is nothing better to strengthen muscles and build cardiovascular stamina than wind sprints. Start them in spring training or your preseason equivalent and continue them all season long.

The goal in wind sprints is to elevate your heart rate to 75 percent of its maximum and maintain it at that level for twenty minutes. In attempting to elevate my heart rate, I will sometimes run with a stopwatch and check my pulse rate below my right ear. I simply count the number of beats, hopefully fifteen beats, in a six-second period and multiply by ten for the number of my beats per minute.

A typical wind sprint is run in the outfield from one foul line toward center field, an approximate distance of seventy-five yards. In twenty minutes, you can usually complete about fifteen to twenty sprints. As your starting day approaches, you may wish to cut the number of sprints to ten or fewer. After you complete a wind sprint, jog at least part of the way back to your starting position so you don't reduce your heartbeat unnecessarily. The way to determine your normal working heart rate is to apply this simple formula: Subtract your age from the number 220 and multiply that sum by .7 or .8. It is rare when anybody, even an athlete, achieves 75 percent of the heart-rate capacity, but it is a goal to work toward.

As in the work with small weights, be honest with yourself. If you are fading out at the end of the sprint, don't jog to the end of the allotted distance. Try a shorter distance that you can complete at maximum speed with maximum effort.

Unless you are a sprinter as well as a pitcher, you may find wind sprints a vexatious task. Make it more fun by competing with a teammate. But, as always, exercise within the limits of your capabilities.

That is my running program. But Steve Carlton, for instance, does no running at all because of a chronically bad back. Other pitchers will do many sprints on the day that they pitch. Be flexible in your running routines as well as in your weight work. Listen to advice from trainers, coaches, managers, and teammates and then decide if it makes sense for you. Only by experimenting will you know for sure what works for you, so don't be afraid to try something new.

Don't forget that maintaining strength and flexibility in your arm and legs throughout the entire year is an absolute of pitching preparation. Look at how many older pitchers are still performing excellently in the big leagues today. To name only a few, there are Steve Carlton, Ferguson Jenkins, Tommy John, Jerry Koosman, Phil Niekro, Nolan Ryan, and Don Sutton. Look also at the continuing excellence of Darrell Evans, Joe Morgan, Graig Nettles, and Lou Piniella. The recently retired Carl Yastrzemski played beyond his forty-fourth birthday. All these contemporary players have absorbed the wisdom of staying in baseball shape virtually all year round. That's baseball shape, not the muscle building you need for weightlifting. Don't confuse one with the other.

Now let us look at how a professional pitcher goes about the specific task of preparing for an individual start: the absolutes of game-day preparation.

GAME-DAY PREPARATION

There is nothing quite like the feeling of expectation on the morning of the day or night that you are scheduled to pitch. As a professional competitor, I believe that you should have some butterflies and healthy tension before you go out on the mound. You may risk staleness and flatness in your pitching if the adrenaline is not flowing.

Like so many aspects of the art of pitching, how you prepare will vary with each individual and will change for each individual over time. Early in my career, I often got psyched up for my starts days before I was scheduled to pitch. Now that I have the responsibilities of raising a family, and have years of experience to call on, I can channel my mental readiness into a period just a few hours before the start of a game.

Sleep and Eating

Ideally, you should get between eight to ten hours of sleep the night before you are scheduled to pitch. But for the professional, the real world of home and road complications often conspire to keep you from getting enough rest. Try to plan to get maximum rest on the second night before your start so your body can build up some of its rest requirements.

If you are pitching a day game, have a good, balanced breakfast: for instance, juice, eggs, bacon, and a couple pieces of toast, or an English muffin, and milk. Adults can have a little tea or coffee. Don't eat another meal after breakfast, although some nonsugared liquids or a little fruit won't hurt you.

If you are pitching a night game, your big meal should be in the middle of the afternoon, no later than 3:00 P.M. A high-protein meal of meat and potatoes, a slice of bread, with plenty of garden greens and vegetables is a good pregame meal. Some carbohydrate buildup in this meal is a good idea, although you don't have to ingest the vast amounts that marathon runners require.

Again, the individual is the important aspect. Keep a daily chart of food, sleep, and exercise along with a chart of how you have pitched. Soon you'll be able to determine which routine is best for you.

Ball Park Routines on the Day of the Game

Before even picking up a ball on the day I'm scheduled to pitch, I run through the series of exercises demonstrated on pages 42 through 51. These exercises, held for five to six seconds and repeated three to four times, gently stretch the major muscle groups that will be called upon once I start throwing. The series begins and ends with a slow jog across the outfield.

You must know your opponent: Part of your mental preparation has been to follow the box scores to see who has been hot and who has not. If you notice that there are strange names in your opponent's lineup, it is your job to ask your teammates if they have played against the newcomers and if they have any tips on what kind of pitches work best against them. Team meetings of pitchers are usually held only before the first day of a season's series against a team, so you must be on top of the situation. If you're playing a team with players who have joined it in midseason, you have to take the initiative to ask for opinions and experiences regarding batters who are unfamiliar to you.

As you prepare to dress for your big challenge, let me say a few things about what kind of equipment and clothing you should use. This may seem like a little thing, but if you are not comfortable and efficient on the mound, the big things like pitching prowess and strategy can be seriously impaired.

Your Uniform

Your arms and your entire body are extremely active while you're on the mound. Your uniform should allow you to perform easily and gracefully. It should not be so loose that it flaps around your arms and legs. It should not be so tight that it constricts your normal movement.

I remember being fortunate while a student at USC to have box seats to a Los Angeles Dodgers game on a night Sandy Koufax was pitching. In those days, pitchers warmed up in front of the dugout. I noticed that early in his warm-up Sandy, a southpaw, pulled the left side of his shirt about two inches outside of his belt. He did not want the shirt to restrict the extension of his throwing arm. I have since used this tip when warming up with my right arm.

It is important to keep your arm and back warm when you are pitching. In addition to my uniform shirt, I always wear a T-shirt underneath. If it is warm, I wear a short-sleeved cotton shirt. If it is cooler, I wear a woolen undershirt. If it is very cold, I wear a long-sleeved woolen undershirt in addition to a cotton T-shirt.

You should change your undershirts every two or three innings. Perspiration can help to cool you off, but you don't want sweat to be absorbed into your shirts. You should probably change even more often in colder weather when a sweaty undershirt can become clammy and chilly. You also want to keep the sweat from rolling down into your palms.

I use the body lubricant Albolene to keep my arm and back

Exercise 1. Upper-body stretches are a series of loosening-up exercises. Begin with giant windmills. Swing your arms freely in full circles alongside your body. Next, reach back with your left arm and swing your right arm freely across your body, twisting your trunk. Then reach back with your right arm and swing your left arm across your body. Then exercise both arms simultaneously. Repeat.

Exercise 2. The first two photographs demonstrate exercises that stretch the latissimus dorsi muscles. With your hands above your head, stretch first to the right and then to the left. The last four photographs demonstrate trunk twisters that stretch your body through a three-hundred-sixty-degree circle. Start the circling in any position that feels comfortable to you, then repeat the circle in the opposite direction. Note that I raise my arms for balance when stretching backward.

Exercise 3. Leg stretches strengthen the hamstring and calf muscles in the trailing leg. Step forward with your left leg and place your hands on your knee. Keeping your back as straight as possible, raise and lower your upper body over your bent leg. Repeat. Then step forward with your right leg and repeat the exercise.

Exercise 4. Assume a squatting position. Stretch your right leg to the side and gently stretch away from that leg. Repeat. Return your right leg to the squat position, stretch out your left leg, and repeat the exercise.

Exercise 5. These are modified windmills. Start by bending at the waist. Touch your right foot with your left hand, then your left foot with your right hand, twisting your trunk from side to side. Next, reach forward and place your hands flat on the ground. Stretch. Then grab your ankles, stretch, and hold. Repeat.

Exercise 6. These are variations on the hurdler stretch. Sit flat with your legs extended in front of you and your feet together. Reach and grab your toes with both hands. Hold for five to six seconds, release, and repeat. Next, spread your legs. Keeping your legs flat, grab your right knee with both hands and lower your chin as close as possible to your right leg. Then grab your left knee and repeat the exercise. Finally, bend forward and grab both ankles, gently stretching and holding five to six seconds. Release and repeat.

Exercise 7. These are groin stretches. Sit flat. Keeping your back straight, draw your feet up as close as possible to your body, soles together. With your elbows and forearms, slowly push down on your knees. Release and repeat.

Exercise 8. Full hurdler stretches are good for stretching both the quadricep muscles of the trailing leg as well as the hamstring muscles of the front leg. Sit flat. Starting with your left leg in the front position, slowly lower your head as close as possible to your knee. Hold five to six seconds, release and repeat. Then stretch your right leg to the front position and repeat the exercise.

Exercise 9. This is the pretzel, which stretches the lower and upper back muscles. Sit flat. Keeping your back straight, slowly turn your head toward the right, look over your right shoulder, and hold for five to six seconds. Repeat. Then look over your left shoulder and repeat the exercise.

Exercise 10. These are crossovers. Lie flat on your back with your arms stretched out, palms up. Raise your right leg and cross over your body to your left hand. Then raise your left leg and cross over your body to your right hand. Repeat three to four times.

Exercise 11. These are modified crossovers. Do these the same way as for crossovers, but tuck your legs up close to your body and roll from side to side toward your outstretched hands.

Exercise 12. Achilles stretches are the last exercise I do before taking a slow jog across the outfield. Standing about three feet from a wall, bend from the waist and lean into the wall. Keeping your body weight forward, bring your right knee in and forward, straightening the left leg until you feel tendons tightening. Repeat the exercise with your left knee forward and right leg back.

protected from the cold and wind. Other pitchers regularly use an analgesic to keep themselves warm.

The only exception to the basic rule "Keep yourself and your arm warm" is when you are playing in sizzling heat. In those circumstances, cooling off your whole body may save you from heat prostration. Hit the water fountain often, not for big amounts of water but for repeated intakes of small amounts of liquid. A Gatorade type of fluid can also serve this purpose.

Your Shoes

Selection of your baseball shoes is obviously a very important decision for a pitcher. The shoes will stretch during the course of a season or more of use, so choose a size smaller than your street-shoe size. Ferguson Jenkins has sometimes pitched in shoes one and a half sizes smaller than his normal walking shoes, but as I have said before and will say again, do not imitate a hero or idol. Make your decision based on how *you* feel.

Because baseball shoes have spikes, they can feel uncomfortable until they are molded to your feet. When trying on a new pair, be sure you are wearing the socks that you will use during a game. I play with two pairs of white sanitary socks that come up over the knee. Other players use sweat socks in addition to the sanitaries.

Once you have selected your shoes, break them in slowly. Wear them to the point of being uncomfortable and then change to your old shoes. Once in your new shoes, you will get the feel of what I mean. Maybe use them only for batting practice or for half of batting practice to avoid getting blisters. Use a shoe-stretcher if you want them a bit wider. If you get blisters, see your trainer or a physician.

When your shoes become old, don't throw them away. They may come in handy for use on a rainy, muddy day. Shoes are expensive and it makes a lot of sense to save a pair of old mudders for use on inclement days.

In the early days of my career, I used a toeplate on the tip of my right shoe. For a right-handed pitcher, the right foot is the power foot, the one that turns off and on the rubber with every pitch and the one you explode off with when you come forward in your delivery. A toeplate saved the leather in those days and was much easier and cheaper to replace than an entire shoe.

Today, the soles of most baseball shoes are made of plastic and a toeplate cannot be fitted to the plastic bottom of the new shoes. We major leaguers still use metal spikes so we are able to get a firm feel for the ground when we throw. There is a liquid compound that can be applied to the tip of a plastic shoe to serve the function of a toeplate. (Available at sporting goods stores, this compound resembles a thick shoe polish and hardens underneath and on top of the shoe toes into a hard glossy coat.) Again, using a compound in this way will help preserve your shoes and save you money in the long run.

Your Cap

A cap should fit comfortably and securely on your head. Most caps today come with sweatbands. If you don't have one, get one for the obvious reason that you don't want perspiration rolling down your face and onto your hand.

Your Glove

The selection of a glove is another major decision. An important part of the paraphernalia of pitching, your glove should be large enough to enable you to hide your pitch grips from the batter and his coaches. It should not be so big as to throw off your balance when you need to make a quick move as the fifth infielder on the defense.

I prefer a firm and secure glove that I can manipulate easily and through which I can feel the ball with my fingers. I don't like a loose and floppy glove, but this is my preference. You must find out for yourself what works for you. Try on as many gloves as you need to, and remember not to let a hero dictate your style. A young pitcher should not buy a glove simply because it is a Tom Seaver, a Nolan Ryan, or a Steve Carlton model. Imitation is not always flattery in pitching, especially if your physique and style are different from those of your hero. Only by trying on a lot of gloves and sensing what feels best for your own hand will you come to a decision on the right kind of glove for you.

Understand that a glove must be suited to your motion and to your fielding capabilities. A glove that is too small for you will hamper your ability to knock down the ball and make important plays. A glove that is too large may throw off your pitching rhythms, one of the worst curses to befall a pitcher. In short, make sure you control the glove and the glove doesn't control you.

There are many ways of breaking in a glove; there is no single unfailingly correct method. I never use any kind of glove oil because it seems to me to make the mitt heavy and less firm. But other players and pitchers like to use a variety of oils, including Lexol. A recent fad has been to apply shaving cream with lanolin oil to the pocket of the glove.

I do advise that you break in a glove slowly. Play catch with it several times in pregame warm-ups before you trust it to a game situation. You don't need a new glove every year if you take care of it. Learn how to relace it. With proper care, the same glove can be used for years. I divide my gloves into gamers, used only for my thirty-five or thirty-six starts a year, and others, which I use for outfield catch, shagging during batting practice, and pepper exercises.

Warming Up for Your Start

The time for combat, "show time" as some of my livelier colleagues might put it, is near. If you are pitching at home, head down to the bullpen about thirty minutes before game time with your bullpen catcher. Carry your warm-up jacket to keep yourself warm after you are finished. Either in the bullpen or beforehand in the clubhouse, do some preliminary warm-up exercises and stretching. Also jog a few light wind sprints to get your circulation going.

The length of your warm-up depends entirely on your individual makeup and the weather conditions. On a very hot day, you may get ready in twelve to fifteen minutes. It may take a little more than twenty minutes on a cold day, especially if you are a slow starter. But never warm up too much. Don't go to the mound exhausted.

If you're playing at home, try to finish your warm-up pitches about five minutes before you're scheduled to start the game. This pause will nearly simulate the interval between half-innings during a game. The sooner your body gets prepared for the rhythm of the game, the better it will function. Don't go to the mound in need of a five-minute break because you started warming up too late.

If you're pitching on the road, make sure you allow yourself enough warm-up time, because the game starts when the home pitcher is ready. Know when the game is scheduled to start and allow yourself sufficient time to get loose.

I learned this lesson the hard way one evening some years ago in San Francisco's frigid Candlestick Park. Fellow USC graduate Jim Barr was pitching for the Giants and I assumed he needed fifteen to twenty minutes of warm-up. I was uncertain as to whether the game started at 7:30 or 7:35, and instead of finding out for sure, I waited until Jim was ten minutes into his warm-up before starting to throw myself.

Imagine my surprise when I discovered that Jim was ready in ten minutes and the game was about to start! Never did I warm up so quickly. Although I wound up sufficiently loose, I vowed never again to allow the opposing pitcher to dictate my own warm-up habits. Know when the game is supposed to start and plan your warm-up around that, not around your opponent's routine.

What kind of procedure should you follow in your warm-up? There is no absolute here; individual style will determine your best method. My preference throughout most of my career had been to start by throwing easily to my catcher while standing on the bullpen mound. He would set up in front of the plate fifty feet away from me, and then slowly retreat backward until he might be as far as seventy feet from the rubber. These warm-up throws might take five minutes.

In recent years, I have preferred a simple game of catch off the mound. I find that these days I can stretch my arm more off the mound. The initial warm-up distances and time allotment remain the same: from sixty to seventy-five feet for about five minutes. There may be slight variations in this procedure depending on my physical condition, the weather, or the particular game ahead. The point is not to follow my routine but to realize that your bullpen time should be used to prepare you physically and mentally for the challenge and joy of pitching.

Once you begin throwing on the rubber, I recommend throwing fastballs alone for the first few minutes. It is your most important pitch, as I will hammer home a little later, and it's good to get it cranking early. Since your breaking and change-up pitches will only be effective if you create the illusion that the fastball is coming, it is important to establish your fastball motion early in your warm-up.

After about five minutes, you can start throwing your other pitches. I recommend trying the different pitches in sequence. For instance, after three fastballs, try three curves. Then return to three fastballs and crank out three changes. Or try three fastballs and three curves and repeat this sequence before trying three fastballs and three changes. Return to the fastball regularly to maintain the fastball motion and rhythm or you are bound to struggle.

I have learned not to trust my stuff in the bullpen as a guide to how well I will do in a game. If you are a positive-minded competitor, your warm-up time is certainly a hopeful time, but don't be overly influenced by what happens in the bullpen. Warming up is when you establish your delivery, making sure it is regular and rhythmic with each pitch.

It may be helpful to ask a batter to stand at the plate in the bullpen while you are finishing your warm-up. Mike Cuellar of the Orioles used to have a hitter stand at the plate all the time while he was warming up. You never really follow through and drive your lower body at the plate unless a batter is standing there, and his responses to your pitches may give you an idea of how your pitches are acting that day. To repeat, though, don't get too carried away by the bullpen reactions, either your own or the batter's.

One final routine may help your bullpen work. You may want to devote your last few pitches to a run-through of all your pitches. Ferguson Jenkins has used this method for years. Just remember that your main job in preparation is to loosen your arm and establish the necessary physical rhythms and mental attitude to do your job.

Setting Up Shop on the Mound

You are now just eight warm-up pitches away from beginning work. You have completed your physical preparation from the day following your last start to warm-up this day in the bullpen. You are mentally ready to face your opponent, knowing what to expect from his capabilities and understanding just what you have to accomplish to defeat him.

I truly believe that when you step out to your workplace, the mound, what has happened thus far in the game is immaterial. If you are on the road, and your team has scored six runs in the top of the first, you still have nine innings to face. If your team is in the cellar or fifteen games out of first place in the standings, that, too, should have no effect on your attitude and preparation.

You stride to the mound, or you may want to trot out there. Before you begin warming up, you should check the footing all around the mound. Even in your home park, you never know when loose footing or some little pebble might suddenly appear and cause a damaging bad hop against you. On an alien mound on the road, you most certainly need to investigate the playing surface.

Get the feel for the pitching rubber, which lies in the center of the ten-inch high mound. Check the footing in front of the rubber and off to the first and third base lines. Any wet spots or soft footing can throw off your delivery, landing point, and follow-through.

On rainy, muddy days, be especially thorough in sizing up the mound before you begin to throw. Your opponent will be hurling under the same conditions, but perhaps he will not be as careful. You may gain a vital edge by knowing more about the surface than he does.

If you are not satisfied with your own efforts, call on the umpire to bring out the groundskeepers, who with rake and drying compound will do a more professional job of preparing the mound area. If your spikes are getting filled with mud, use a tongue depressor to get the clumps out of your shoes.

There is a resin bag to the side of the rubber. Some pitchers use it to keep their hands from getting sweaty. I rarely use it, but I make sure to put it behind the rubber, well out of my range of motion. Putting the resin bag out of harm's way is just another little practice that can help a pitcher keep his work habits orderly and precise.

You can now begin your official warm-up pitches. You have an allotment of eight pitches. Toss the first couple easily, not at full speed. Then begin to deliver the ball as you would in the game, beginning with the fastball, then mixing in breaking pitches.

The eighth pitch is usually a fastball. You indicate that it is your last warm-up toss by making a flipping gesture with your glove toward second base so your catcher will know to throw to second after he receives the ball. Your infielders will then throw the ball around the infield before returning it to you.

You are now ready to go to work. For nine innings, a starting pitcher hopes to be the master of the show. He knows that the batters will in all likelihood get some hits off him, but he strives to make them happen in harmless places. To succeed and to maintain your success over the years in the game of baseball, you need to learn the absolutes of pitching mechanics.

3 THE ABSOLUTES OF PITCHING MECHANICS

How many times have you heard people rave about some pitching prospect's "great arm" and "overpowering stuff"? Yet the pages of baseball history are filled with stories of pitchers who never lived up to their potential. If successful pitching were simply a matter of raw ability and great pop on a fastball, the roster of Hall of Fame hurlers would be far longer.

I believe that the secret to pitching mastery and longevity lies in understanding and applying the absolutes of pitching mechanics. Most likely, the great talents who failed to fulfill their promise did not understand the basic principles of the mechanics of pitching. There will be exceptions to the absolutes explained in this chapter. Pitching remains an expression of individual style and, many times, a gifted pitcher can use his own physical idiosyncrasies to bend one of the absolute rules. But if you strive to compete consistently and durably as a major-league hurler, I urge you to understand and to apply to the best of your ability the following lessons.

The basic principles are simple and commonsensical. The art of pitching requires the coordination of the entire body, top and bottom, left side and right side. If you want to analyze a pitching motion like a clinician or just a fascinated fan, visually divide the pitcher at the waist. Watch his lower body and watch his upper body and see how they work together. Then, mentally divide the motion into quarters so you can observe his right leg and left leg and his throwing arm and his gloved arm separately and together.

It is imperative to pitching success and durability to incorporate the lower part of your body—your thighs, your buttocks, and your back—into your motion. Your arm and shoulder are frail and delicate compared to the weighty muscles of your lower torso. You get your strength and your stamina from the lower body. Those muscles provide the support with which your arm can throw pitch after pitch throughout the years of a professional career.

Absolute Number 1: Keep the Front Leg Flexible!

The key to incorporating the lower body into the art of pitching lies in flexibility of the legs, especially the front leg: the left leg in a right-handed pitcher and the right leg in a left-handed pitcher. After nearly two decades of major-league experience and close observation of my fellow moundsmen, I cannot emphasize enough how important a flexible front leg is to an aspiring pitcher. If you keep your front leg stiff while delivering the baseball, the lower half of the body works against the upper half. It is likely that in a few years the only delivery you will be capable of is the mail delivery.

Name me any sport in which flexibility is not an absolute necessity, whether it be football, basketball, tennis, or racquetball. Whereas a right-handed pitcher derives his power from his rear right leg, the left leg bears the brunt of every pitch as it is released. The more flexible that front leg can be trained to be, the less the strain you will place on your delicate shoulder and arm muscles.

It may be easier to throw with a stiff front leg. It takes a lot of concentration and much more physical effort to incorporate your lower body in every pitch. You may even have thrown several no-hitters in high school and shutouts in the lower minor leagues off a stiff front leg. Ultimately, however, the odds on injury to your upper body, especially your arm and shoulder, will increase.

One of the most dangerous side effects of throwing off a stiff front leg is the bullwhipping reaction of your throwing arm. I remember when I joined the Cincinnati Reds in 1977, my teammate Tom Hume had the stiffest front leg I had ever seen.

After each pitch, his arm bullwhipped—coiled back on itself—like a rubber band that had been snapped violently.

Tom had been plagued by frequent arm soreness, so he was ready to listen to my advice. Like most mechanical adjustments, the change was only slight. I recommended that he keep his weight on his right foot throughout most of his motion so he could land more flexibly on his left foot. Because Tom had gotten into bad habits, he had to work very hard to make the adjustment to good habits. But he improved dramatically and has risen today to the stature of one of the National League's best relief specialists.

Craig Swan was another pitcher afflicted with a stiff front leg. When he joined the Mets in 1973, I watched him closely. One day I warned, "Craig, if your left leg doesn't become more flexible, some day you may break your arm." I hadn't meant this literally, but a few months later, Craig walked into the locker room with his arm in a cast. His bad mechanics had caused a stress fracture in his elbow. Through a lot of hard work and rehabilitation with Met trainer Larry Mayol, Craig worked his way back to major-league fitness.

I advise young and aspiring pitchers: Don't wait for an injury before developing proper mechanics. Perfect good habits early in your career. The longer you retain a bad habit, the more difficult it will be to break and correct that habit.

A pitcher should be a creature of habits, as many positive habits as possible. In the middle of a game with vital pitch decisions to make every few seconds, you shouldn't be consciously worrying about mechanics. You want to have good mechanics mastered so you can concentrate on the mental aspects of pitching. You can't face a hitter like Dave Parker, for instance, worrying whether or not your knee is too high in the stretch position. At those times when the game is on the line, you want to possess good habits so that the mechanics can take care of themselves. A good pitching coach will be able to spot a flaw in your mechanics and tell you what you're doing wrong. If your basic mechanics are sound, you will be able to correct that flaw immediately.

There are, of course, exceptions to the rule of the flexible front leg. Milwaukee's Don Sutton and Montreal's Steve Rogers both pitch off stiff front legs. But I believe that in a sense these outstanding pitchers prove the absolute rule, because neither

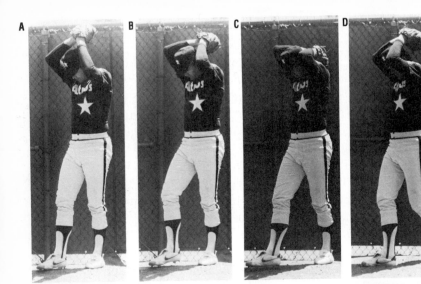

A B C D E F

L M N O

Nolan Ryan is an excellent subject for the study of good pitching mechanics. His arms and legs, his upper and lower body—the halves and quarters of the body that I have talked about—are wonderfully coordinated. Notice how Nolan's front leg is flexible from the very first photo and how he keeps his head down (**A** through **F**) in an attempt to keep his weight as far forward as possible.

Beginning with **I**, he has clearly picked up his target at the plate and he begins to collect himself for the thrust and delivery of the pitch. Notice how well he has hidden the baseball as he reaches the apex of his knee lift (**I** through **K**).

As he reaches into his glove for the baseball he turns his glove wrist inward, keeping his left shoulder, hip, and knee closed until **P**. Nolan rotates his shoulder on a horizontal plane (**T**). (Compare this to the forty-five-degree angle established by Steve Carlton in **R** on page 79.) He has tremendous flexibility in his left leg and maintains that flexibility throughout the delivery and follow-through (**Q** through **X**). Note also the outstanding external rotation in his rotator cuff in **S**. He releases the baseball from an excellent angle of delivery outside his right ear (**S** and **T**). At the end of his follow-through, his throwing arm has completed its arc to the outside of his left leg (**X**).

U

63

Steve Rogers has a somewhat unorthodox, stiff-legged delivery, but he demonstrates that there are many paths to pitching success if you are creative and consistent in your efforts. He achieves tremendous hip rotation, generated by the turning of his left knee at the height of his lift (**H** through **J**). Steve hides the ball very well and keeps it invisible to the batter until very late in his delivery (**Q**).

He has excellent left-arm action. He turns his left wrist inward and keeps his left side closed (it doesn't begin to open until **P**) as he prepares to bring the ball into throwing position. He squares his shoulders toward the plate very well (**Q**), if not exactly establishing a forty-five-degree angle, coming reasonably close to it. He does not have the flexibility in his landing leg (**R**) that Nolan Ryan or I have, but he compensates by completely following through with his arm toward the left side of his left leg (**T** through **V**).

bullwhips his throwing arm after the ball is released. Each makes sure that the right arm follows through across his body toward and past his left hip. Both players realize the importance of removing as much strain as possible from the pitching arm. They understand that the more time the arm takes to decelerate, the less violent the strain will be.

Like great artists and writers, great pitchers usually develop an individual style. Don Sutton and Steve Rogers have been creative enough to adjust to a motion that is ultimately more effective for them. Young hurlers should never imitate the exceptions but absorb and follow the rules. As the English teacher said to the pupil who wondered why Hemingway could use "ain't" and he couldn't, "When you get to be a genius, you can break the rules." At the outset, master the fundamentals.

I assure you that if you follow these rules of pitching mechanics, you will be able to throw as hard as you throw now for a longer period of time measured in innings per game, starts per year, and seasons per career. Good mechanics will improve your control and thus increase the chances of lengthening your career. Let me now take you step by step through the mechanics of pitching.

Standing on the Rubber

The pitching rubber is a slab twenty-four inches long and six inches wide. You throw every pitch off the rubber. Get the feel of it with your foot and make sure that it is smooth. When you decide what is the best and most efficient place for you to start your motion, make sure that you use that starting point for each and every pitch. The essence of good pitching is deception. Don't give the hitter an advantage by standing in one spot for a curveball and a different one for a fastball. Remember that every move you make on the mound registers in the mind of the batter. Good hitters especially will take advantage of any tips you are inadvertently giving them.

There is a classic story about Babe Ruth suffering a mound slump during his first career as a pitcher. The batters were teeing off on Babe's deliveries and he was terribly frustrated. Then, a coach pointed out to Babe that he was sticking his tongue out every time he wound up to throw a curveball. Babe corrected that flaw and had an outstanding pitching career before he transformed baseball as a slugger.

Most right-handed pitchers toe the rubber to the right of center. I find my best starting point to be equidistant between the center and the right end of the rubber. I place the front part of my spikes on the front edge of the rubber. Nolan Ryan has a similar starting point. We find that standing toward the right of the rubber enhances the angle of our fastballs and breaking pitches.

A notable advocate of a different position was the San Francisco Giant Hall of Fame right-hander Juan Marichal. Juan used to stand at the extreme left edge of the rubber. He felt that his wicked screwball broke best from that position, into the right-handed batters and away from the left-handers.

Juan, of course, had one of the most spectacular front-leg movements in baseball history. But don't go to the mound trying to imitate him. Find the spot from where you feel your pitches work best and stick to it.

Receiving the Sign

As I toe the rubber with my right foot, I place my left foot approximately a half-step in front of me. I have found that if I place my left foot behind my right one, my weight is shifted too far to the rear as I go into the windup. I want to keep my weight forward so that I can pivot on top of my power foot, the right foot.

Nolan Ryan also keeps his left foot in front of his right foot as he prepares to start his pitch. He bends down to receive the sign to insure that his weight is forward. I receive the sign in a straight-up position, but I am mentally aware of the need to keep my weight forward on the right foot.

There will be many variations in positioning the left foot while taking the sign from your catcher. As long as the principle of keeping your weight in front of the rubber is understood and followed, the placement of the left foot is not especially important at the outset of your motion. You may find that keeping the left foot even with the right foot or a half-step behind works best for you.

Get a Comfortable Starting Position

As in all the areas of nonabsolutes of pitching, experiment to discover your most comfortable starting position. Nolan angles his feet slightly while I keep mine straight. Try a few different positions to see which works best, but once you decide the proper placement for your feet, be sure that they remain the same way for every pitch.

Absolute Number 2: Rub Up the Baseball

One of the great charms of baseball for a pitcher is that you can determine your fate. If you do your job well, the offense can be stymied and frustrated. In no other sport does the defense control the ball. That's why good pitching is the key to winning baseball games. It all starts with you standing alone on the mound with the stitched sphere of a baseball.

It is your responsibility to make certain that every baseball you throw feels comfortable in your hand. Each ball is slightly different: On some, the seams are higher and on others they may be smoother; some may feel larger and some may feel smaller. You don't know exactly how a given baseball will feel until you take the time to rub it up.

Before each game, professional umpires rub up the baseballs with a special kind of mud to remove some of the gloss. When the ump throws a new baseball out to you, you must take the time to rub it up again. You must treat the baseball with the same kind of care you have given to your glove, your shoes, and your other equipment.

Rubbing the ball creates friction and the heat generated from that friction brings the oil from the hide to the surface of the baseball and increases the tactile sensation in the hand and fingers. Rubbing off the gloss on the ball may also serve a very practical function. Breaking pitches have been known to hang when thrown with unrubbed baseballs. A pitcher will say, "It just slipped out of my hand at the last second."

Rubbing up the baseball can also have a safety benefit. I recall one game during my career when I didn't rub up the ball as carefully as I should have. The ball was hit to an infielder and resulted in a putout at first. When I received the ball again, I noticed a little needle sticking out of one of the seams! We were all lucky not to have been injured that day, but that rare incident has always served to remind me of the importance of rubbing up the baseball.

Absolute Number 3: Hide the Baseball!

The competition between batter and pitcher can often be decided on little edges a pitcher may unknowingly give a batter. One of the grave mistakes of this kind is tipping off your pitches. Instead of a hurler hiding the baseball in his glove, keeping the ball out of the batter's line of sight until the last possible moment, he openly spins or fondles the ball in his throwing hand. A left-handed hitter may gain a great edge on a right-handed pitcher (or right-handed hitters on southpaw hurlers).

Even if the hitter cannot see the ball, the third- or first-base coach can relay to the hitter what the pitch is if he can see the ball behind your back. If you or a teammate notice a coach bending over every time you throw a breaking pitch and staying upright on every fastball you throw, you are probably allowing him to pick up your pitches. There's a sick feeling in having a hitter drive a good pitch out of the park when you get the sensation he knew what was coming. Avoid such dismay by practicing this absolute of pitching mechanics: *Hide the baseball!* You will see many pitchers in the big leagues who don't abide by that maxim, but I don't know of many outstanding and consistent winners who defy this rule. The Yankees' fearsome reliever, Rich Gossage, keeps the baseball visible, but most batters know his fastball is coming anyway. I see many pitchers in the major leagues today who fail to properly hide the ball in their throwing hands. It is a bad habit that may have proven too difficult for many to break. If you insist on showing the ball, at the very least make certain that you hold it in the same way before you put it in your glove and start your pitch.

Positioning the Glove

The best way to hide the baseball is to place it in your glove before you begin your windup. The glove can rest at your waist or your chest or somewhere in between, which is what I prefer and Nolan Ryan does, too. The important point, again, is consistency. Always position the glove in the same place for each and every pitch.

Also make sure that you reach into the glove for the baseball at the same point for each pitch. If you reach into the glove later for a curveball than you do for a fastball, good opposing coaches

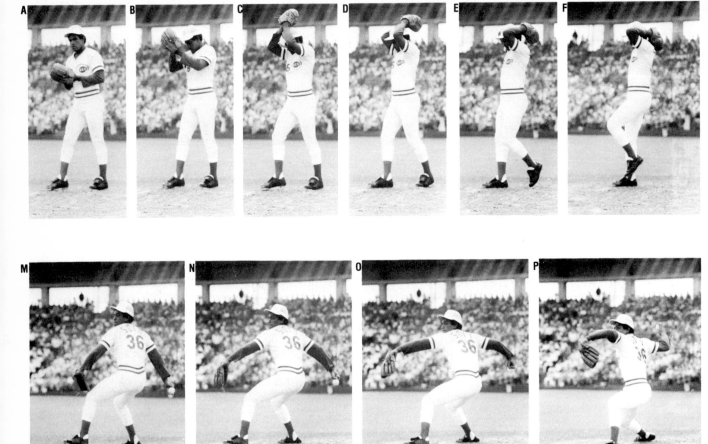

Mario Soto demonstrates excellent mechanics from start to finish. He hides the ball in the glove so that the batter does not even glimpse it until late in his delivery (**Q**). He very fluidly coordinates his knee lift with the breaking of his hands (**F** through **K**). He demonstrates excellent extension of the left arm, which pulls down and enables the right arm to come up into throwing position (**L** through **Q**).

He keeps his left side closed until he is ready to come forward toward the plate with his pitch (**R**). He demonstrates excellent flexibility in both his landing and pivot feet (**N** through **V**). Notice the right angle that his legs establish and maintain as he explodes toward the plate (**S** through **V**).

The baseball should be in the same position in your glove before each pitch.

You should enter the glove with your hand at the same position for each pitch.

Correct way to enter the glove for a fastball.

Incorrect way of entering the glove: Too much skin is showing from the end of your sleeve as you enter the glove.

Incorrect way of entering the glove: You can see the ball being gripped as you stand at the plate.

Correct way to enter the glove for a curveball: The ball is hidden from the batter and his baseline coaches, so they can see no difference between your curveball and fastball grips.

will soon be tipping off the hitters. Before long, all your opponents will be drooling with expectation at your pitches.

I recommend the following mechanics for entering the glove. When you place your hand in the glove, make certain the wrist of your throwing hand rests in the same position for every pitch. Your right hand should reach in for the ball at the point where the heel of your glove might be taking your pulse. A cautionary note here: Be aware that should you ever accidentally drop the ball while your foot is on the rubber and you have a runner on base, you will automatically be charged with a balk.

I also recommend that pitchers only use a closed-web glove. The open "H-web" type of glove does not hide the ball entirely and you may tip off your pitches that way.

One last point on glove placement. Many pitchers and fielders keep the index finger of their gloved hand outside their glove. They may find that the shock of the ball arriving in the glove is less painful with the finger outside the glove. I would not utter an absolute warning against this practice, but there are two reasons why pitchers should think twice before they acquiesce to this fashion.

First, your finger can be more easily broken if it is sticking out of the glove. Second, you could be tipping off your pitches by the movement of that exposed finger on your gloved hand. Good coaches and observant teammates can tell you if you are giving away your pitches. Ask them to be alert to inadvertent clues.

Choosing the Windup

The windup is the synchronization of individual parts of the body in preparation for driving the ball through the strike zone. There is certainly no absolute way of winding up to throw a baseball. Everyone's physique is different. Everyone's timing is slightly different, too. Since pitching is such an act of individual expression and creativity, windups will vary greatly.

The important point on the windup is to find an efficient and effective style and to use it consistently. Like everything else with mechanics, you want the windup to be identical for every pitch. Obviously, if you pump more on fastballs or change your motion for curves, the batters will soon gain an unwholesome edge on you.

Your physique will play a major role in determining the kind of windup to use. A tall pitcher like Jim Palmer, with long arms and legs, can pitch effectively with a big windup. On the other hand, if you are shorter-armed, an elaborate windup could lead to trouble, disrupting your coordination and timing. Remember that a windup is only an appetizer, not the meal. You should not fall in love with a motion that is not best for you. Like the backswing in golf, the windup is a prelude to power, not the power itself.

At the other extreme from the picturesque windup is the no-windup motion that became popular after Don Larsen pitched a perfect game with it in the 1956 World Series. There is less danger of breaking your rhythm and your tempo with the no-windup, but you may find that the absence of a windup prevents you from injecting the maximum amount of energy into your pitch. This has been my experience. A no-windup motion doesn't work for me because, from a timing standpoint, I cannot coordinate all the parts of my body in such a short time.

I utilize instead what would be called a limited windup. This is a motion suitable for my physique, which, unlike the angular physiques of Jim Palmer and Ferguson Jenkins, is more heavily

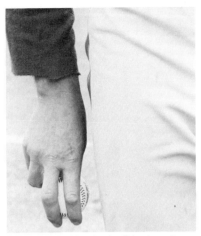

Failure to hide the ball in the glove: A fastball grip is given away.

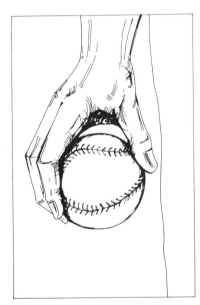

Failure to hide the ball in the glove: The entire side of the ball is visible and a curveball grip is tipped off. If you have developed the bad habit of fondling the baseball outside your glove, at the very least try to roll the ball the same way before each pitch to prevent your grips from giving away your pitches.

muscled, especially in the lower body. I bring my hands back in a small pump before reaching into my glove for the ball.

The Weight Shift and the Breaking of Hands

As your windup starts, your weight for the only time during the entire delivery of a pitch shifts to the rear. The left foot in a right-handed pitcher (right foot in a left-handed pitcher) is brought back perhaps a half-step behind your right foot in back of the rubber. The exact rhythm and balance in your motion will only come with practice and more practice. Learn to be aware of the moves you make when you are most successful. Strive to educate your muscles to know when that correct feeling has been established. Through practice and repetition, it will become second nature to you.

As you begin to shift your weight backward, you reach into the glove for the baseball. You must decide at what point to break your hands. There is no absolute rule here. Experiment with different points until you feel that you are operating at maximum effectiveness. I tried breaking my hands both behind my head and above my cap until I settled on a spot in front of my face. Every pitcher will have to determine the right position by experiment, but there is one general rule to use as a guide: Try to break your hands over the top of your lead knee.

Absolute Number 4: Get It Out, Get It Up!

If there is no absolute method for breaking the hands, I do recommend the absolute wisdom of a phrase taught to me by Harvey Haddix, my first pitching coach in the big leagues and the man who once pitched twelve innings of perfect baseball only to lose the no-hitter and the game in the thirteenth inning. Harvey declared, "Get it out and get it up!" He meant that a pitcher must get the ball out of his glove and into throwing position quickly.

There is obviously nothing to be accomplished by keeping the ball in your glove. If you are slow bringing your pitching hand up into throwing position, your arm will lag behind your body and throw off your timing. Coaches like to use the expression "He's having trouble getting his arm up" to describe a fatiguing hurler. Pitchers can battle this dangerous tendency by constantly remembering Harvey's positive little adage, "Get it out and get it up!"

I cannot overemphasize how important these seven words are to successful pitching. You are at a critical juncture in the delivery. For the only time, your weight has partially shifted behind the rubber to your left foot. You are breaking your hands preparatory to bringing the arm up into throwing position. Don't dawdle or fumble in the glove. Get it out and get it up!

Eyeing the Target: Focus Point and Target Point

One piece of time-honored advice to pitchers has been, "Keep your eye on the target at all times." Pitching coaches urge their charges to concentrate on facing home plate. It is a commonsensical principle akin to driver-education teachers telling their pupils to look in front of them to make sure that the car doesn't swerve.

Having established and endorsed the general principle, let me confess that I do not always follow it. I keep my head down from the moment I receive my catcher's sign until I am ready to end my windup and throw the baseball. I have found from experience that I am not effective when focusing on a general area like home plate or the center of the catcher's mitt.

I deviate from the norm because experience has taught me that I have trouble keeping my weight forward on my pivot foot when my head is up throughout my entire motion. Therefore, I pick a preliminary "focus" point lower than my eventual target point. This focus point may vary with different pitches and different kinds of hitters. For instance, I may pick up the belt buckle of a right-handed hitter who crowds the plate or the right elbow of a left-handed hitter who stands back in the batter's box.

I do not recommend my particular variation to a young pitcher. Most established winners keep their heads in front of them facing the plate at all times. I have made my method work for me because as I go into my delivery I have already determined the point I will pick up, and when I do pick up my target, that is all I see as I begin to deliver the ball. I also maintain the cardinal rule of all pitching mechanics: consistency with each and every pitch. Regardless of your target or focus points, if your head moves differently with different kinds of pitches, you again face the danger of tipping off what is coming.

The Knee Lift

One of the most dramatic parts of any pitcher's motion has been generally called the leg kick. Juan Marichal possessed perhaps the most sensational left-leg motion of any right-handed pitcher in baseball history, and Warren Spahn had a great right-leg motion for a southpaw. But I feel that the term "leg kick" is a misnomer. It should be called a knee lift. Its purpose is to provide momentum for the drive to the plate. But you must stay in balance when you kick, keeping your left shoulder level and nearly parallel to the ground and your weight solidly on your right foot.

One of the big problems for young pitchers is that they kick their lead foot too high and throw the top half of their bodies backward and out of rhythm. Instead of driving their bodies toward the strike zone, they fall off in one degree or another to the left side of the mound. In the enthusiasm of youth or from competitive zeal, pitchers sometimes fall into the trap of thinking that muscling the ball to the plate will substitute for good mechanics and rhythm. The earlier you learn the folly of this viewpoint, the quicker you will become a pitcher and not just a thrower. My former Met teammate Jerry Koosman, still going strong at the age of forty, established himself as a winning left-handed pitcher when he mastered an efficient right knee lift where previously he had kicked his front leg without adequate control.

Jim Palmer has suggested that a good guide to a proper knee lift is if you can freeze your motion at the height of the lift. If you fall over backward or cannot maintain your balance, then you must make an adjustment. If you can hold the knee in position, you will likely have achieved the desired balance to continue on with a successful motion.

Make sure that you lift the knee to the desired height with every pitch. Here, too, you want to avoid tipping off pitches with different knee lifts. Inability to raise the lead leg to its usual height is a telltale sign of fatigue. If the knee is low, the arm will be "behind," out of rhythm with the rest of the body. You begin to sling the ball instead of driving it toward the strike zone. Be wary of fatigue; it leads to bad mechanics that inevitably cause sore arms.

A final absolute regarding the mechanics of the left side of your body is to keep your shoulder, hip, and knee "closed," that

Steve Carlton demonstrates a classic delivery, utilizing every advantage that his six-foot-five, two-hundred-twenty-pound frame and exceptional strength provide. Notice that beginning with **B**, his left leg is already flexible, although he has not yet begun to turn. Like Nolan Ryan, Steve Carlton starts his motion with his head down, helping to keep his weight forward. Beginning with **D**, he has brought his head up and picks up his target. He is a picture of fluidity and coordination as he attains his maximum knee lift (**D** through **H**). He gets excellent hip rotation that provides exceptional energy for his pitches. He keeps his right shoulder, hip, and knee closed until he is ready for the delivery to the plate. His shoulders establish an excellent forty-five-degree angle (**L** through **N**).

He lands flexibly on his right leg (**P**) and he easily follows through with his arm toward the outside of his right leg (**U** through **W**).

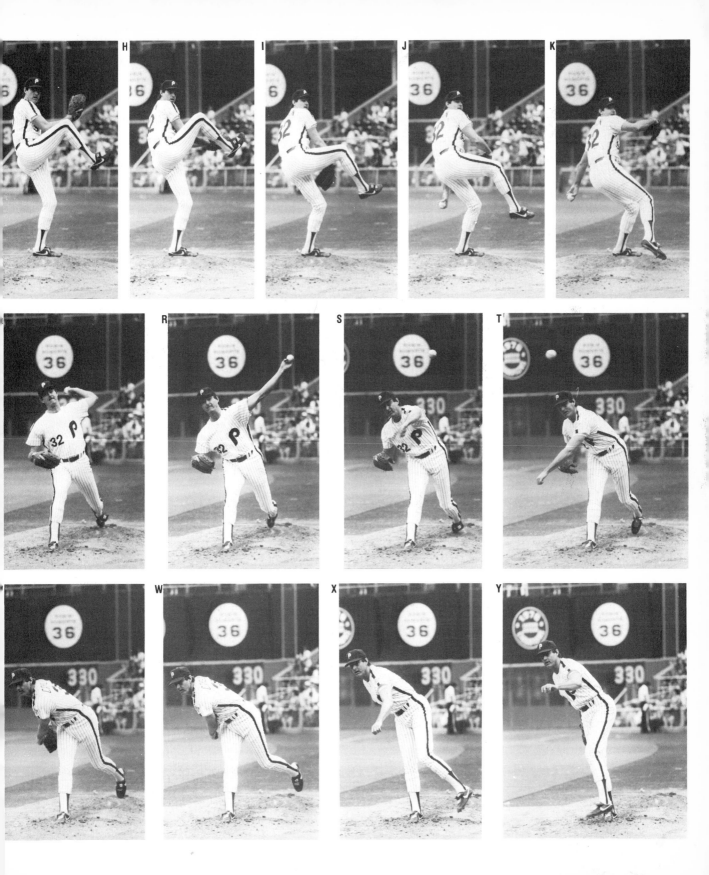

is, not facing the plate. Closing the left side provides a formidable barrier to the batter's vision of the forthcoming pitch and you will have momentum directed to the plate when you do open up.

Rotation and Thrust of the Right Side

As your lead leg lifts, your body begins to rotate on the pitching rubber, becoming coordinated for the final moment of delivery. To achieve maximum momentum with each pitch, you must turn toward third base. How far should you rotate? There is no absolute here; your physique and how your body feels will dictate what works best for you. Some people have said I turn so sharply that I thrust my back uniform number into the batter's line of sight. But I certainly don't rotate as much as Luis Tiant used to, or as Gene Garber, the Atlanta Braves' stellar reliever, does today.

The important thing is to get ample hip movement into your rotation and thrust. You generate a lot of power from your hips in pitching as well as batting. Utilizing hip movement is an important aspect of pitching as long as you keep your balance by maintaining your weight on top of your pivot foot.

A right-handed pitcher gets power from the right side of his body while the left side, especially the left leg, absorbs the brunt of the delivery. As you begin to deliver your pitch, the right side dips slightly to the rear, which increases the distance your arm will travel and thereby increases your arm speed. While I do not recommend that all pitchers keep their right side as low as I do—angular pitchers would find that difficult—I stay low and "drop and drive" toward home plate because I am trying to drive the ball low through the strike zone with as much controlled energy as I can generate. I try to maintain flexibility in both legs by keeping each leg bent at the knee. I generate power by exploding off the rubber with my right foot. If you want to throw hard and effectively, you must push hard off the rubber. You don't have to imitate the grunt I sometimes make when I am releasing the ball, but you do have to remember to be ready to give it your all when you release the baseball.

The Stride

The stride for a right-handed pitcher is the distance between the right foot on the rubber and the left foot when it touches the ground at the end of the knee lift. There is no absolute distance that a pitcher should stride in the process of throwing the baseball. In the bullpen before I warm up, I use this method: I place one foot in front of the other, touching, and pace off shoe-lengths. My stride distance is five and a half shoe lengths.

Whatever method you devise is fine so long as you keep your stride consistent. It will maximize deception and minimize potential injury. The stride should not be so far as to inhibit flexibility in the legs. If you overstride, there is no way that you can effectively utilize the strength and cushioning support of your lower body.

The magic time for delivery has arrived. You have worked at coordinating your body movements; now is the moment when your pitching ability comes to the forefront. You have lifted your left knee and taken the ball out of your glove and brought it behind you. There is no absolute rule as to how far you should bring the ball at this stage except to remember Harvey Haddix's dictum to get that ball up into throwing position as soon as possible. I am most effective when I bring the ball behind my right leg so that it almost scrapes the ground, trying to attain a maximum controlled arc for my arm.

My lead foot hits the ground at the end of the knee lift with my left toe pointing toward home plate. I am ready to bring the ball forward to its release point. "Show time" has arrived. Where is the best point to release the baseball?

A useful illustration for understanding release points is to envision a clock over the pitcher's mound. If you are a batter, the most severe overhand thrower will come at you from twelve o'clock. But to throw directly over the top is virtually a physical impossibility given the curve of your arm and shoulder and the turning motion involved in pitching.

Most pitchers, including me, deliver the baseball from a three-quarter, or ten or eleven o'clock, position on the dial. The exceptions to this rule are the sidearm specialists who deliver from the nine o'clock position. They can be extremely difficult to hit, especially lefty sidearmers for lefty hitters and righty to righty. Sidearm pitchers usually have trouble throwing breaking pitches and changing speeds because the plane of release is so flat. But such creative pitchers as Kansas City's Dan Quisenberry and Pittsburgh's Kent Tekulve have made names for themselves and helped their teams by mastering this particular style.

I would urge young pitchers to try to master the basic principles of three-quarter overhand pitching. If you can be deceptive and make batters *think* you are coming sidearm, so much the better. Long, lanky Don Drysdale used to convey the impression of dropping down sidearm to right-handed hitters when, in fact, he was still coming largely from over the top.

As you release the ball, from whatever spot on the dial, you must follow these basic principles: (1) Your fingers must be on top of the ball. After much practice, your arm and shoulders will come to know this feeling. Your fingers are on top and you are driving the ball on a downward plane through the strike zone. If your fingers are not on top of the ball, either because of fatigue or lazy mechanics, your arm is behind your body. Your fingers accordingly fall to the side of the ball. This is the place where "hanging" pitchers are born. (2) Your elbow must be above your shoulder to insure that you achieve the downward plane through the strike zone. Aim to establish a forty-five degree angle from the release point behind your right ear to your follow-through point at your left hip.

You must work constantly to perfect the exact release point. If you are too close to your ear, your hand may be inside the ball instead of on top of it. If your hand is too far outside your ear, you run the risk of gripping and throwing the ball from the outside instead of on top. You must stay on top of the ball and maintain an angle approaching forty-five degrees downward. There will, of course, be individual variations in obtaining the optimum release points.

Establishing an effective release angle will require devoted individual effort. But you cannot go wrong if you follow the basic principles of keeping your fingers on top of the ball and your elbow above your shoulders and bringing your arm down at a forty-five-degree angle to your opposite hip. These are principles that apply to Phil Niekro's knuckleball as well as Nolan Ryan's Express fastball, because the difference between a flutterball and a high-speed hardball is only forty miles per hour, microseconds in the real world of mound life.

Aim to establish as wide an arc over the top as you can efficiently achieve. The wider the arc, the more velocity and movement you will get on the ball. Consider the analogy of racing cars on a speedway oval. The car on the outside of the track generates more momentum than the inside car because it is traveling across a wider arc. So will your arm generate more speed if you establish a wide but efficient arc.

Experiment with different release points. Work between starts in the bullpen with your coach. Ask for opinions on whether you are maintaining the same (or very nearly the same) release points for all your pitches to maximize your deceptiveness.

If you have mastered the basic mechanics, establishing an effective release point should be a satisfying touch for you. It is the moment when your individual ability asserts itself. Robin Roberts used to say that he could almost see himself delivering the ball and hear his wrist pop at the moment of release. The release point is when, in Roberts's immortal words to a rookie roommate on the Orioles, Jim Palmer, "you throw the hell out of the ball."

Incorporating the Gloved Hand

The left arm is essential to a successful right-handed pitching motion. It acts like a rope to lead the right side of the body toward home plate at the completion of delivery.

As you begin the windup, the left arm is extended and rotated inward. As you deliver the ball, uncoil your left arm, pulling down with your elbow at a forty-five-degree angle past your hip. Driving your left arm down outside your left hip at this angle, as though you were trying to knock the wind out of someone standing behind you, will help establish good off-arm mechanics. Pulling with your hand rather than your elbow will cause you to sling the ball. Once again, looking in a mirror will help. As you uncoil the left side, pulling down, the left shoulder comes down and the right shoulder goes up, increasing your arc. You are thus generating more energy to put behind the ball.

Try to avoid a left-arm movement horizontal to the ground. If you rotate into your delivery with your left arm horizontal, your throwing arm and your pitches will be "flat."

Try not to let the left arm go behind your body. If you possess the kind of delivery that pulls your gloved arm behind you, you must be diligent at getting the arm back in front of you as quickly as possible. Remember that your gloved hand is your first line of self-defense as well as a valuable ally in fielding.

You may also want to flick your gloved hand into the batter's line of sight with every pitch. It can disrupt the batter's timing slightly but significantly. Jim Palmer is a master of that quick glove flick.

Coordinating both arms in pitching is vital to your success. I often draw an analogy to prizefighting. If you wanted to knock someone out with a right-hand haymaker, you would bring your left arm out and up first. That is precisely what you should aim to do in right-handed pitching. Use your left arm as a guide and a pulley to prepare your right arm for its explosive journey through the strike zone.

Follow-through and Landing

Pitching, like all athletic movements, cannot be completed successfully without an effective follow-through. If you don't continue with your motion after you release the ball, your arm will have slowed prematurely and your pitch will suffer in the Big Three areas: velocity, movement and location. Cutting short your follow-through leads to bullwhipping your arm and will increase the potential for injury.

Your pitching style will determine the kind of follow-through you employ, but there are two absolutes in following through: (1) Your glove must be in front of you as the first line of self-defense and for fielding readiness. (2) Your legs must be bent. You may have noticed the smudge of dirt on the right kneecap of my uniform. That is always a good sign to me that I am driving down when I release the ball and am incorporating the powerful muscles of my lower body. Remember, the more your legs are bent, the more your lower body is absorbing the strain of pitching and conserving your arm and shoulder. A follow-through as close to the ground as mine may not be effective for you. Develop your own style. I would certainly not recommend Bob Gibson's violent follow-through where he seemed to fall off the mound with each pitch. But it worked for that Hall of Fame pitcher, who possessed such quick reflexes that he was also an excellent fielder. Find what works best for you with experiment and practice, always bearing in mind the absolutes of self-defense, fielding readiness, and flexibility in the legs.

Your goal in landing should be to arrive slightly on the inside ball of your left foot with your toes pointed toward home plate. A perfect mechanical landing may be hard to achieve because of the complex nature of pitching with all its coordinated movements. What you should avoid at all costs is landing on your heel. A heel landing will cause your leg to stiffen and produce the undesirable side effect of bullwhipping your arm. If you land pointing toward first or third base, you will also increase the stiffness of the left leg, leading to more wear and tear on the arm.

A proper landing will allow you to maintain body balance and rhythm. It will bring to the end of your motion the kind of proper form you strive for from the moment you start to wind up. It will aid your consistency and durability. If you find that you are landing on the outside of your lead foot, you can correct this flaw by slightly pushing the left knee inward as you go into your landing position.

Working from the Stretch

The only difference between the windup and the stretch position is that you turn your body sideways to the plate and you rest your pivot foot (the right one for a right-hander) on the front edge of the rubber, using the right side of your foot for contact. The left foot is parallel to the right about a half-step in front of it. You bring your hands to a full stop in the stretch position between your chest and your waist (at whatever position works for you). The purpose in stopping is to keep the base runners from running wild on you.

Otherwise, pitching from the stretch position involves the same principles we have discussed. You must hide the ball from the batter, and you must reach in for the ball with your wrist taking the pulse of the heel of your glove.

The stretch position causes psychological tension in many young pitchers because of the apparent danger of runners on base. It took Sandy Koufax, for instance, years to master the stretch motion. Once he caught the knack, it helped his maturity as a dominant pitcher. Soon he had mastered his stuff so well that he didn't have to pitch from the stretch very often.

In the last few years, I have noticed that many short-relief specialists like Bruce Sutter have taken to pitching from the stretch even with no runners on base. This may be useful to young pitchers who know they will be pitching a lot of relief. It will enable them to get comfortable in the stretch position when

Many young pitchers forget that pitching from the stretch requires the same sound mechanics as working from a full windup. In this sequence, once I have established my set position at the waist (**A** and **B**), everything is identical to a regular windup motion. I keep the ball hidden in my glove and then by my left knee so that the batter does not see it until **R**.

I quickly bring my hands up into throwing position by **J**. If you have trouble getting your hands out of the glove in the stretch, practice at throwing them up to get yourself into good pitching rhythm. I establish a good forty-five-degree angle between my shoulders by **O** and when I land in **P**, I establish and maintain a flexible left leg. My throwing arm follows through nicely toward the left side of my left leg (**U** and **V**).

there is no danger on the base paths. They will then feel confident when a team is threatening with men on base.

I often see young pitchers dawdle in getting the ball out of the glove while they are in the stretch position. They forget that a key to effective pitching is rapid, coordinated movement of the hands from the glove through the backswing to the release point to the plate. "Get it out and get it up!" applies to the stretch position as much as it does to the windup. If your arm is lazy or slow from the stretch, one way to correct that is to throw both your hands up together at the same moment as you begin your knee lift.

You may want to lower your knee lift a little in the stretch to keep the base runners from getting too big a lead on you. But you still must get both your knee and hands up quickly to prepare your throwing arm for the release.

Try to keep the base runners honest. Don't let them get a walking lead on you. Decide on an imaginary point—perhaps the grass edge on dirt or turf infields—past which you will not let a runner go before throwing to first base. Give your catcher an honest chance to throw out a potential base stealer.

On the other hand, don't overdo concentration on the base runner. Remember that you had your chance to get him and didn't. The batter on the plate should be your primary concern. Don't live in the past, trying to make up with a pick-off what you didn't do with a pitch.

The Commonest Mechanical Flaws

In pitching as in life, we may strive for perfection but rarely attain it. Fleeting glimpses of Nirvana soon evaporate. Baseball is, after all, a game of hits and runs—and errors—and poor pitching sometimes cannot be avoided. There are, however, many common flaws that can be corrected.

(1) Rushing is every pitcher's biggest nemesis. You are competitive and you want the ball to arrive at the plate quickly and deceptively. But don't make the mistake of thinking that the speed and power of your body will equate to the velocity and movement of the pitch. In fact, a rushed body without the proper timing leads to a lagging arm and ultimate injury—not the goals of your choice.

Rushing usually occurs when your weight is not balanced. You may be thrown off by keeping your weight too long on your left foot as you go into your windup. Or you may have toppled toward the right while rotating on the rubber with your right foot. Whatever the cause, rushing results in poorly directed pitches, frustration, and even worse, injury. No pitcher ever waited too long to synchronize his upper and lower body before throwing the ball.

(2) Overthrowing often occurs at a critical moment in the ball game. Or it may occur at the start of a game that you want to win badly. You put too much into your arm movement, forgetting that you pitch with your body and don't merely throw with your arm.

Overthrown pitches are usually high and in the batter's wheelhouse (that area of the strike zone where the batter likes the ball), proving again that wise axiom of pitching that "more muscle is often less result." You cannot pitch effectively with tense muscles, especially the forearm muscles that are usually the culprits of overthrowing.

(3) Throwing across the body results when your legs become unsynchronized. Instead of landing with your front foot to the left of an imaginary line from the center of the rubber to the front of the pitching mound, you are landing to the right of the line. Since your left leg is landing off line, your back leg will also come down awkwardly. You cannot utilize your lower body effectively in the thrust and the follow-through, and you subject your throwing arm to dangerous wear.

There are no easy ways to cure these bad habits. I fight rushing all the time. I often say to myself, "Do not rush! Do not rush!" before I release the ball. You may have seen the famous pictures of Don Drysdale grimacing before he released the baseball. He was not trying to intimidate the batters, although that may have been a desirable side effect. He was reminding himself not to rush but to complete his fully balanced motion with his left side closed until the moment of release.

As for overthrowing, you can conquer that excess of enthusiasm by simply telling yourself to relax and allow your good mechanics and proper delivery to assert themselves. If you get beat with your best pitch, that's life. Goose Gossage relaxed himself before he threw the final pitch to Carl Yastrzemski in the 1978 Yankee-Red Sox Eastern Division pennant play-off game by telling himself that the worst thing that could happen to him was that he'd be skiing in his beloved Colorado mountains the next day.

Drills to Improve Mechanics

Many common mechanical flaws can be corrected with specific drills. A pitcher with the raw physical equipment, the mental awareness, and the spiritual desire will find these helpful. A young pitcher may be lucky enough to have a close working relationship with a pitching coach who can supervise these drills and provide sympathetic and critical advice.

I am happy to see that many major-league organizations now provide a pitching coach at virtually every minor-league level. The art of pitching is complex and requires a willingness to engage in a lot of arduous trial-and-error experimentation. The more good advice young pitchers receive, the earlier they will attain pitching maturity. Providing minor-league pitching coaches is a reform long overdue.

(1) Overstriding occurs when a right-hander steps out too far with his left foot. He usually lands on his heel, and his right shoulder does not come across in its proper arc.

The drill to correct overstriding involves placing a towel, resin bag, or glove (something soft), perpendicular to the pitching rubber at the point where your left toe has been making contact with the ground. Then, gradually, inch by inch, move the object back toward the rubber until you reach the optimal landing spot.

(2) Throwing across the body can cause career-ending injuries if it is not corrected. In recent times, Don Gullett, the stellar southpaw for the Reds and the Yankees, had a brilliant career curtailed because he could not correct this flaw and caused major damage to his left arm and shoulder. Durable pitching requires that your legs and arms work together, that you land with your lead foot underneath your lead arm and your pivot foot underneath your throwing arm. Steve Carlton's classic mechanics illustrate the point graphically and explain why he has had such consistent success.

To eliminate the dangers of across-the-body throwing, place a soft object—again, a towel, glove, or resin bag—perpendicular to the pitching rubber, starting at a point where the inside of the left foot comes in contact with the ground. Inch by inch, move the object back toward the rubber until the landing foot is at least at the center of an imaginary line running from the rubber to home plate. The ball of your left foot ideally should land just to the left of center of that imaginary line. You don't want to land too far to the left, because then you are opening up too much.

(3) A lazy gloved arm must be corrected if both sides of the body, arms and legs, are to be coordinated for a successful pitching delivery. If you have a particularly lazy off-side, non-throwing arm (and trainers will tell you that this arm is often weak in pitchers because they think it is not important), try this drill.

Drop to your knees in the outfield and lob the ball to another player about thirty feet away. Slowly back up—still on your knees—until you are about forty feet from your partner. You can't use your lower body while on your knees and will therefore develop the proper forty-five-degree angle with your left arm and knee. Once you've worked in the relaxed surroundings of the outfield, you should be able to return to the mound with renewed confidence.

(4) Lack of control is a common problem of youth. Coaches often ask me for advice on cutting down the wildness of young pitchers. I suggest that the hurler limit himself to throwing fastballs in practice (his most important pitch, anyway, as we shall shortly see) and aim at a stationary catcher. Practice, practice, practice, using either the catcher's left knee or right knee as the main target.

If you watch me pitch, you will notice that I constantly converse with my catcher and occasionally with my infielders. There are many things you simply cannot observe while on the mound, especially after you have completed your follow-through. Where did the batter make contact? Where did your motion go awry? How did the ball move? These are only some of the questions that your teammates can help you with. Remember that you are one of nine players on the defensive team. As pitcher, you are the leader, but you are all in the fray together. Consult them when in doubt. Ask for their opinions, though understand that you remain the final judge. You should develop the confident feeling that you are the master of your fate on the mound.

There is no substitute for practice and desire in mastering these absolutes of mechanics. After you have achieved a level of experience and success, you may wish to alter some of these basic rules as several of my accomplished contemporaries like Don Sutton and Steve Rogers have been able to do. But the rules of incorporating the lower body into your delivery and keeping your elbow up and your hand on top of the ball remain absolute for all pitchers.

The art of pitching is in finding that blend and sequence of pitches that will continually keep the batter off-guard. Keeping in mind the absolutes of pitching mechanics, let's look at the pitches in a major leaguer's arsenal.

4 THE FASTBALL

I enjoy giving baseball clinics where I can expound and exchange ideas on pitching. Shortly before spring training began in 1983, I addressed a gathering of high school and college baseball coaches in Tarrytown, New York. I decided to start the proceedings with a teaser for the assembled experts. I asked, "What is the most important pitch in baseball?"

I got a lively response. "Slider!" boomed a few voices. "The fastball!" rejoined others. A lover of the high hard one yelled, "Strikeout pitch!" There was a smattering of support for specialty pitches like the forkball and the knuckleball. After listening to the various opinions, I said, "The most important pitch in baseball is the fastball."

I then posed another question: "What is the second most important pitch in baseball?" Everybody had an opinion on this, with more votes for sliders, curves, change-ups, forkballs. A wise guy in the back even shouted, "Spitter!" After listening for a while, I said, "The second most important pitch in baseball is the fastball."

The fastball is the cornerstone for the foundation of the art of pitching. Rube Walker, my former Met pitching coach who is now with the Atlanta Braves, used to hammer home this homily about the fastball. I have never forgotten it. You cannot possess effective curveballs, sliders, or change-ups if you have not established the preeminence of your fastball.

If you look through the pages of baseball history, you will see that nearly every outstanding pitcher had and used an effective fastball. The era doesn't matter. Walter Johnson and Rube Waddell early in the century, Lefty Grove and Bob Feller later on, and closer to our time, Don Drysdale, Bob Gibson, Sandy Koufax, and Juan Marichal all had effective fastballs. The pitchers participating in this book—Steve Carlton, Steve Rogers, Nolan Ryan, and Mario Soto—all have and use superior fastballs.

Sandy Koufax once said, "The art of pitching is the art of instilling fear." He was not being malicious. He simply meant that a pitcher cannot be afraid to throw his fastball on the inside corner of the plate and, occasionally, between the corner of the plate and the batter.

The inside fastball is the pitch that will establish the outside corner for you. The batter cannot dig in on you if he knows that you are willing to throw inside, into what we call in baseball his "kitchen." Your fastball is the best way to establish that you are the boss and that he, the batter, must be on the defensive.

I hate to see young pitchers with great arms and good stuff fall in love with sliders or other pitches. If you have a good hummer and don't throw it at least 60 percent of the time, you are doing your team and, more importantly, yourself a disservice.

A good fastball is a God-given gift. Through correct mechanics you can improve your natural ability, but the pop and movement is something you either have or you don't. Baseball scouts look for a certain minimum velocity and movement on a fastball when they sign prospects. The fastball is the pitch that can open the door to pro baseball, and then the pitching hopeful forgets to use it.

I will always be grateful to Ernie Bowman, a minor-league teammate, for a piece of advice he gave me one day. A former utility infielder for the San Francisco Giants near the end of his career with the Jacksonville Suns in 1966 as I was on my way up to the big leagues, Bowman came to me on the mound and said, "Kid, you got a good fastball, but to keep it, you gotta throw it. Don't save it for Christmas." Sure, batters will occasionally hit your hard one a long long way, and sure, you need breaking and off-speed pitches to break a hitter's timing. But the old number one, the fastball, remains the best way to establish your domination of the hitters.

Sometimes, in a game where you have a comfortable lead, you may want to test a dangerous hitter by giving him an accessible fastball. It is a way of feeding information into your computer for future use in a game that may be closer. For instance, I remember once trying a high and inside fastball on the Giants' slugger Darrell Evans. I had a comfortable six-run lead that quickly dropped to five when Darrell belted it into the upper deck in San Francisco, but I learned something about Darrell's power zone that I could later put to use.

You don't have to possess Nolan Ryan's supersonic velocity to throw an effective fastball. Remember what I said at the outset: Every pitch has three dimensions—velocity, movement, and location—and if you don't have the last two, all the velocity in the world won't help you. Tommy John has had an outstanding career in both major leagues by changing speeds on his pitches and throwing a deceptively moving fastball with excellent control. He has proved (and so did Eddie Lopat of the Yankees in an earlier generation) that you can win in the major leagues with a fastball clocked at under eighty-five miles per hour. But you must control it, and most of all, you must *throw* it. "Don't save it for Christmas."

You shouldn't worry if a hitter occasionally belts one of your fastballs over the fence. You must accept the humbling truth that good hitters will sometimes hit your best pitches. You cannot let an occasional setback deter you from applying one of the most vital principles of pitching: Establish your fastball as a constant reminder to the hitter of what you are capable of doing.

The fastball can be effective thrown for strikes and, as deception, outside the strike zone. The inside fastball is especially valuable when it forces the batter back from the plate, making it hard for him to reach out for your outside pitches.

You must convince a hitter that he cannot have both sides of the plate. You cannot let him dive out over the plate and connect solidly with your best low and away fastballs or sliders. Somewhere in the sequence of pitches in each game to every hitter, the fastball must be thrown *in*, off the plate, as a message that says, "Don't forget, I might come back in here at any moment." The earlier you establish that possibility, the better.

During games in which you feel especially strong, you may be able to accelerate your fastball from fast to even faster. Juan Marichal once said that a pitcher with two good fastballs

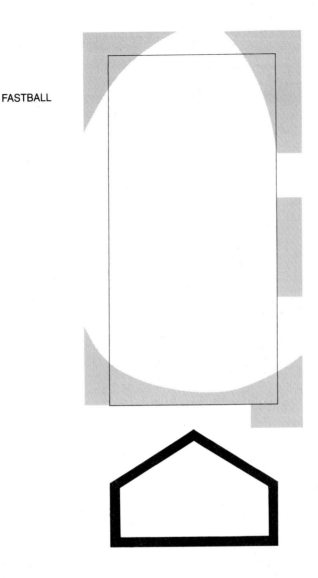

FASTBALL

Areas of the fastball's effectiveness.
The black line represents the traditional rectangular strike zone, the horizontal measurement equaling the width of the plate, the vertical measurement indicating the distance between the batter's armpit and the top of his knee. The shaded areas show where the fastball is most effective.

One of the reasons the fastball is your money pitch is that it can be effective in most areas of the hitting zone. Thrown low, it can be effective the entire width of the plate, including down the middle. It works well to right-handed hitters throughout the inside strike zone or to left-handed hitters on the outside corner. The fastball can be thrown effectively high or low inside to left-handed hitters, and high or low outside to right-handed hitters.

thrown at slightly different speeds would be a guaranteed winner. Nolan Ryan has been blessed with the ability to accelerate his fabulous fastball during the course of a game. Imagine how a batter feels when he faces a ninety-four-mile-per-hour fastball and then a few pitches or innings later, he has to contend with a ninety-eight-mph hummer.

The slight variance in velocity, if the movement and location remain good, can thoroughly disrupt the batter's timing. Remember that the bat may be more than three feet long but there are only about eight inches on the meat of the bat that comprise the danger zone to the pitcher. If the hitter is primed for one kind of fastball and a slightly different one arrives, you may have successfully disarmed him.

Realistically, a pitcher with Ryan's speed and savvy comes along only once a generation, if that. But all aspiring pitchers should learn early in their careers how to vary the speeds on their fastballs. Later on they can work on changing speeds on their breaking pitches. Knowing how to change speeds is virtually a surefire method of attaining and maintaining pitching effectiveness.

Fastball Grips and Pressure Points

There are no absolutes in gripping a baseball for any pitch. The human hand is infinitely variable, and every finger is a little bit different from every other in size, strength, and surface.

The most common grips are either with (along) the seams or across the seams. Like so many aspects of the art of pitching, you will have to experiment to find out which grip works best for you. Try a grip on the small seams, then a grip across four wide seams, then experiment across two wide seams. Somewhere on that ball there is a spot that feels as though it was born to be, the perfect place for your fingers.

On those days when you are not pitching and are just watching your teammates play, hold a ball in your hand as you watch the game from the bench. Feel every aspect of the baseball, get to know what it feels like to hold the ball on different seams and experiment by applying pressure with your fingers at different points on the ball.

Try those various pressure points when you throw. Try using your middle finger as the main pressure point. Then try the same pitch applying pressure with your index finger. Throw the ball with the thumb on the bottom seam, then try the same pitch without using a bottom seam. Apply different degrees of pressure with both your thumb and your forefinger. Most important, observe the results at home plate.

I don't mind repeating here a point I make throughout this book: Don't imitate your heroes in gripping a baseball. There will be great variations in grips. Mickey Lolich, the outstanding Detroit Tiger southpaw who was briefly my Met teammate, used no seams whatsoever in throwing the baseball. He threw all his pitches off different glossy parts of the baseball to maximize the amount of movement that he could get into the ball. Don't imitate him either, of course, but strive to find what works best for you.

Your grip should be effective and efficient. Do not worry if at first a grip feels unfamiliar. If you feel good with the grip but the batters are "lighting" you up all over the ballpark, go back to the drawing board on the sidelines to find a less comfortable but potentially more beneficial grip. You will be surprised at how much more comfortable your hand will feel when batters are striking out.

Just as batting coaches recommend that hitters not squeeze the bat too tightly, pitching coaches usually advise hurlers not to grip the ball too hard. It should lie securely in your hand, and yet if someone firmly tapped the ball, it would fall out. You will get more spin and rotation on the ball with a relaxed rather than a tense hand, but I don't consider this an absolute rule. The game situation and your stuff on a particular day will be the best guide to the intensity of your grip.

There are two basic kinds of fastball, the rising fastball, which stronger pitchers like Nolan Ryan can count on almost every time they're on the mound, and the sinking fastball, which as a general rule can be mastered by those without Ryan's strength. I throw both kinds of fastballs with variations on each, but I recommend that the fledgling pitcher not get too fancy at the outset of his career. Master one kind of fastball first, then gradually increase your arsenal.

Remember that both the riser and the sinker are only as good as the control you can develop for each. Velocity, movement (liveliness), and control can only be attained by practice and by educating your muscles to recognize that special feeling of harmony that occurs when you are pitching correctly.

The Rising Fastball

For the rising fastball, also called the riding fastball, I have a mental image of the course of the ball. There are three elements affecting the ball: (1) its velocity toward home plate; (2) gravity; and (3) the energy of centrifugal force on the ball determined by the amount of backward spin put into the pitch.

The scientific principle that explains why a fastball can defy gravity and rise is called Bernoulli's Law. A long time ago, this Swiss scientist discovered that as the speed around a gas increases, the pressure decreases. So when you unleash a good riding fastball with substantial velocity, the normal air pressure and gravitational force pulling downward on the baseball are momentarily overcome by the sharp rotation and centrifugal force induced by the spinning baseball.

Grips for the Rising Fastball

A common grip for the rising fastball is across two of the wide seams of the baseball. A grip across two seams enables all four seams to be working for you. To the batter, a ball with all four seams turning appears smaller and thus harder to hit. Of course, the ball isn't, in fact, any smaller than for any other pitch using different grips. Believe me, though, if the batter sees a difference, the pitcher has gained an edge in the constant one-on-one conflict that is the heart and soul of baseball.

Both Nolan Ryan and I grip the rising fastball across two of the wide seams of the baseball. We place our index and middle fingers similarly, about a half-inch apart with the stitches under the pads of these fingers. The ring finger and the pinkie are curled on the side of the ball with the thumb tucked underneath on a bottom seam about midway between the two fingers on top.

There are times when I throw my riser without my thumb on a seam underneath the ball. This is another example of not becoming a slave to habit on grips. You must not be afraid to make changes if your results have been mediocre the old way. Conversely, once you make an adjustment, don't be afraid to try the old way again. I always used to throw my riding fastball without a thumb on a seam. Then I went completely the other way, always using a seam. Now, I use both grips.

Ferguson Jenkins even uses different grips on his rising fastball for left-handed and right-handed hitters. He uses the cross-seam grip for pitching to right-handers because the ball tails into them. He uses a grip along the two narrow seams when facing left-handers because the ball jumps into them. But don't imitate either one of us and don't get too fancy with grips. Master one grip first.

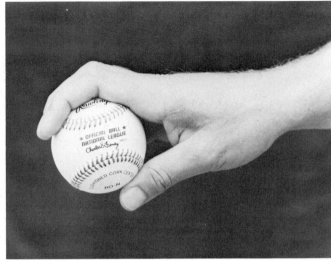

For the riding fastball, I grip the baseball across two of the wide seams with the pads of my index and middle fingers resting on top of the stitches about a quarter to a half inch apart. My thumb is tucked underneath the ball on or near a bottom seam. The ring finger and the pinkie are curled on the side of the ball.

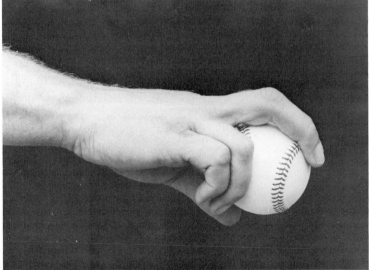

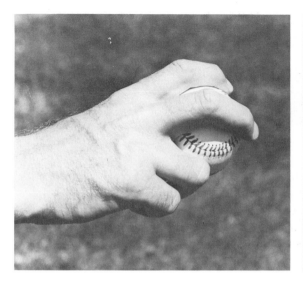

Nolan Ryan holds the ball across two of the wide seams with the pads of his index and middle fingers resting on the stitches. He keeps these fingers more than a half inch apart. His thumb lies underneath the ball with the bottom of the thumb pad resting on a bottom seam.

Steve Rogers grips his fastball with his index and middle fingers about a quarter to a half inch apart across two of the wide seams. The thumb is tucked underneath with the end of the thumb pad resting on a bottom seam.

Mario Soto holds his fastball across the wide seams of the baseball. The pads of his index and middle fingers rest on the stitches of a wide seam with his middle finger slightly in front of his index finger. These fingers are between a quarter and a half inch apart. His thumb is tucked underneath the ball with its pad facing inward off the seam.

Pressure Points for the Rising Fastball

Unlike many power pitchers, I find that my index finger provides a more effective pressure point for my rising fastball than the larger middle finger. For my hand, I get more movement in the baseball off the index finger. In fact, I know at the end of spring training that I am getting ready for the season when a callus forms on the ball of my index finger.

On the other hand, Nolan Ryan throws his marvelous Express with pressure from his middle finger. Jim Palmer and Ferguson Jenkins, outstanding fastball pitchers and authors of pitching manuals, also throw the fastball off their middle fingers.

Practice throwing the ball with many different grips. As long as you stay away from bad habits and maintain good mechanics, you cannot go wrong with whatever grip you decide upon.

Release Points for the Rising Fastball

Recalling the image of the clock from the previous chapter, I recommend that the release point for your riser should be at about the ten o'clock position. Your hand may feel as though it is in a twelve o'clock position with the fingers on top of the ball, and it is to your advantage that the batter think you *are* coming at him from directly over the top. Illusions aside, because of the curve of your arm and the wide arm arc that you should strive to establish, you will actually release the riser behind your ear at approximately ten o'clock.

Just as you should experiment with grips, try many different wrist positions in throwing the fastball. A slight turning of the wrist inward or outward will cause a different movement on the ball. Analyze and cultivate the feeling of that movement. Use it to your advantage when facing hitters who may be sitting on your more conventional fastball.

Your wrist should be relaxed, not stiff. But when it's time to throw the fastball, don't be lazy. Snap your wrist like a whip. The main feeling that you want to develop in throwing the rising fastball is that you are *driving* the ball. Don't guide it to the plate. Drive the ball, with your body under control, through the strike zone.

Remember that old standby, "Keep your fingers on top of the ball." If you stay on top of the ball and drive toward the plate,

Steve Carlton grips his fastball well out in his hand toward the fingertips. He grips the ball with his index and middle fingers close together on two wide seams to enhance the effect of all four seams biting the air. His thumb rests across a bottom seam.

you will maximize both the rotation and velocity of the baseball and minimize the danger of the ball flattening out at the plate, thus becoming easier to hit.

The Sinking Fastball

The sinking fastball, the sinker, is usually a "heavier" ball. That term comes from the ball feeling heavier when the catcher receives it into his body.

The purpose of the sinker is to produce a ground ball by making the batter hit the top half of the ball. When throwing the sinking ball to a right-handed hitter, aim to have him make contact on the thin, handle part of the bat. When pitching to a left-handed hitter, your objective is to force the batter to make contact on the end of the bat as the ball sinks down and away from him. When facing a "dead" pull left-handed hitter, a good sinker on the outside corner is a pitch that will result in a routine ground ball to the second baseman.

I use a common sinker grip, placing the pads of my index and middle fingers along the two narrow seams. The inside of my thumb knuckle rests on an underseam.

Most often, I use my index finger to apply pressure on the sinker, but occasionally I will use my middle finger instead. For instance, if a particular hitter has been very troublesome for me, sitting on my usual sinker, or I definitely need a ground ball for a double play, I will switch to my middle finger for pressure in sinking the ball.

The release point on the sinker is the same as on the riser. Keep your wrist flexible and come from over the top. Again, it may appear as though you are releasing from the twelve o'clock spot on the clock, but ideally you are coming from ten or eleven o'clock. The sinker does not spin as much as the riser because you grip fewer seams and do not apply as much velocity.

Steve Rogers of the Montreal Expos has one of the most devastating sinkers in today's game. He has a natural sink to his fastball, but he has made his sinker even more effective by constantly experimenting with different grips and pressure points. As I do, he usually throws his sinker off his index finger.

Philosophically, the sinker is an excellent pitch for your game plan. It starts low, working away from the red-hot zones where the batter can hurt you the most. Generally, low pitches are

For the sinking fastball, I hold the baseball along the two narrow seams, with the pads of my index and middle fingers resting atop the stitches. The inside of my thumb knuckle rests on an underseam. My ring finger and pinkie are curled on the side of the ball.

One of my variations on the sinker is somewhat like Steve Rogers's grip. I turn the ball slightly on the side and grip it just inside the two narrow seams with my index and middle fingers. I apply more pressure on the outside of my middle finger and the outside of the seam. The effect is to make the ball sink more and move in less toward a right-handed hitter.

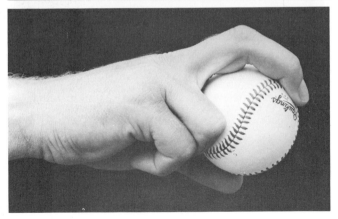

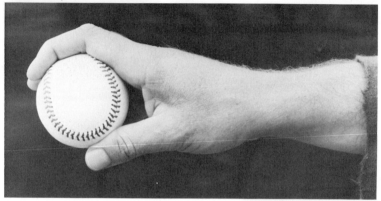

In a third variation on the sinker, I grip the ball on the narrow seams but closer to where the wide seams begin to branch out. This grip tends to give more lateral, rather than downward, movement to my sinker.

Steve Rogers grips his excellent sinker along the two narrow seams. He places his index finger slightly outside one of the narrow seams, with his middle finger slightly outside the parallel seam. His thumb rests underneath on a bottom seam. He finds that his sinker gets the best movement when it is released off his index finger and thumb, with his middle finger applying very little pressure.

Areas of the sinker's effectiveness. The sinker is obviously most effective thrown low in the strike zone. If thrown well, it can work for you even if thrown over the plate. The sinker can contain a right-handed hitter when thrown up to his thigh on the inside corner, or at the equivalent height on the outside corner to a left-handed hitter.

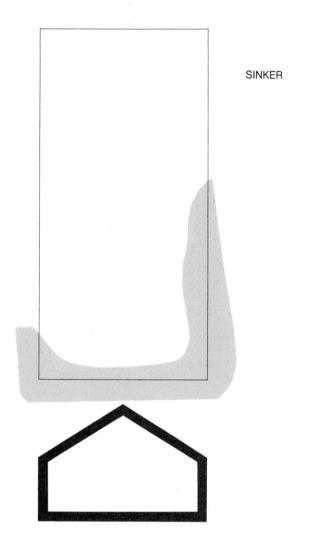

SINKER

most effective because the batter sees only the top half of the ball and cannot hit it squarely.

There are variations on these fastballs that the maturing pitcher may want to add to his repertoire once he has mastered a basic fastball. For example, there is the "turned two-seam fastball" that I use when the good rising fastball has deserted me for a particular game or perhaps just for a few innings in a game.

I call it a turned two-seam ball because I turn the ball a little on its side and apply pressure from the outside of my index fingertip instead from the middle. The effect is that the ball moves low and inside on a right-handed batter and low and away from a left-handed batter.

There is also the sailing fastball that I use to supplement the riser. This pitch is effective up and in to a leftie and up and away to a rightie. I throw it with the four-seam grip but hold the ball slightly to the right of center. This is one pitch where my fingers are not truly on top of the ball.

You hear a lot of TV talk these days about the "cut fastball." This is just another kind of moving fastball that tails away from a right-hand hitter and into a leftie. It looks like a slider but lacks the sharp downward movement of a good slider. It is effective because of its different kind of movement in the hitting zone.

Pitchers experience great joy when their fastballs are humming. "I didn't even feel that one," a pitcher may exult. "It just seemed to jump off of my fingers." The sooner you master the fastball, the quicker you will approach pitching maturity.

Of course, you cannot survive on this one pitch alone, but if you have a live arm and good stuff, you should throw your "number one" pitch—as the catchers signal for it—almost 65 to 75 percent of the time. There are certain weak hitters who never should receive anything but fastballs. They cannot get around on it, and it baffles me why some pitchers throw soft stuff to a batter who might be able to hit breaking balls and change-ups but cannot hit a fastball.

Keeping in mind the primacy of the fastball, you are now ready to look at the theory and the practice of two of the most devilish pitches ever concocted to stymie the life of a batsman: the curveball and the slider.

5 THE BREAKING PITCHES: THE CURVE AND THE SLIDER

Having stressed the supremacy of the fastball, it is important to understand why you need some breaking pitches to increase your proficiency. You can rarely succeed as a major leaguer throwing just your fastball. The hitters are getting paid for something, too—don't ever forget that humbling fact if you are a pitcher!—and sooner or later, they will catch up with your fastball. "Turn up the dial!" is what we say in the dugout to encourage hitters to quicken their bat speed against a pitcher whose only effective pitch is a fastball. Believe me, sooner or later, they will turn up the dial on their bats, and you will be in trouble if you lack the breaking pitches to disrupt the timing of hitters who are sitting on your fastball.

The two main breaking pitches are the curve and the slider. Some pitchers like Nolan Ryan who have great curves don't throw sliders at all. A great pitcher like Steve Carlton throws both curves and sliders. While my slider is generally more effective than my curve, I throw them both.

The purpose of both pitches is *to create the illusion in the batter's mind that a fastball is coming.* If the pitch has a noticeable break on its journey to the plate, the batter's timing will be disrupted and he won't be able to recover in time to hit the ball with authority. The curveball's velocity is significantly slower than the fastball's, perhaps as much as ten miles per hour as measured by our radar guns. A good curve breaks downward between ten and twenty feet from the hitting zone, confounding the hitter who had been expecting a harder pitch in a higher plane.

The slider does not break as much as the curveball. It also starts out like a fastball and appears to be one until it is less than ten feet from the hitting zone. When well thrown, it breaks across the plate and slightly down. The slider has been called a "nickel curve" because the break is less than for the curveball. But it is a very deceptive pitch because the breaking action takes place so near to the hitting zone.

Imagine that you are a batter thinking fastball all the way. You have the meat of the bat poised, ready to connect in a plane for the fastball. Suddenly, the ball moves down and away from you, if you are a right-handed batter (or down and in if you're left-handed). In microseconds, you must deal with a pitch too fast to be a curveball but breaking too much to be a fastball. If it is a good slider, you usually cannot make a successful adjustment.

There's the rub. A poorly thrown slider, the infamous "hanging" slider, can be tagged a long, long way. Proportionately, more home runs are hit on bad sliders than any other pitch. A "flat" slider, thrown with your fingers on the side of the ball instead of on top, lacks all of the Big Three pitch dimensions—velocity, movement, and location. It comes up to the plate with an invitation to long ball written all over it. Moreover, the slider can do serious damage to the arm. While it is easier to throw than the curveball because the velocity is almost as great as the fastball, the slider is especially fatiguing to the elbow and the muscles of the forearms. Unlike most other pitches that spin out of your hand normally with a simple wrist movement, the slider requires a slight pulling down with the elbow at the last fractional moment to ensure that the pitch has that late lateral movement in the hitting zone. I compare the motion to the kind of sharp downward movement of your elbow when you throw the knife into the ground in a game of mumblety-peg. Others have likened the slider's release to the throwing of a football, in which the elbow bears the primary burden of release.

The key point is that throwing the slider can be taxing if you don't have the kind of physical build to withstand the stress. I have always been able to throw it, but I note that the astute Los Angeles Dodgers organization has a policy of restricting use of the slider among its minor-league pitchers to those who have

SLIDER TO RIGHT-HAND HITTER

SLIDER TO LEFT-HAND HITTER

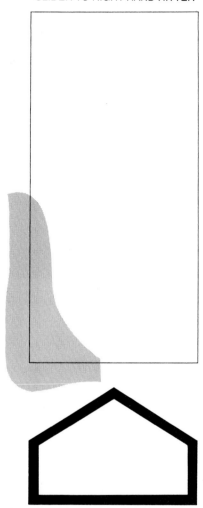

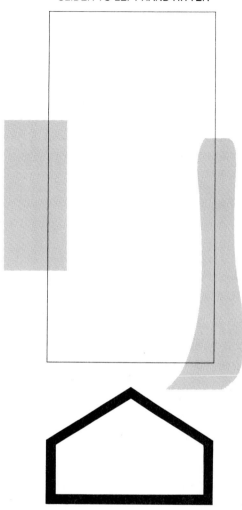

Areas of the slider's effectiveness to a right-handed hitter. The slider is an effective pitch breaking down and away to a right-handed hitter. It works well from the middle part of the plate to, and beyond, the back of the low outside corner.

Areas of the slider's effectiveness to a left-handed hitter. The slider to a left-handed hitter is effective thrown down and away on the outside corner of the plate. It is also effective breaking into the left-handed batter's kitchen, the midsection of his body. This so-called backdoor slider is very effective when preceded by a sinker, because the batter thinks the ball is sinking outside the strike zone and, instead, it slides in toward him.

the physique to throw it without strain. The slider has caused too many arm injuries. Improperly thrown curveballs have also curtailed promising careers.

Nolan Ryan, who throws a great curve but no slider, says that one of the secrets of his success has been that he threw nothing but fastballs until he was twenty-three. It will be interesting to watch the progress and durability of the Toronto Blue Jays' talented young pitcher, Dave Stieb, who, because he was an outfielder until late in college, has not had to contend with the strain of throwing many breaking pitches early in his career.

When a young pitcher begins to learn the curveball, I strongly recommend that he work closely with his coach or someone who is knowledgeable about pitching and that he concentrate on mastering one curve before trying variations. Don't run before you've perfected the mechanics of walking.

George Bamberger, my former Met manager and a highly respected pitching coach, has some very good advice for working with young pitchers. "If a pitcher complains that his curve will never be very good," George says, "have him develop a slider. If his curve is coming along, though, have him stick to that before tinkering with a silder." Just make sure that the breaking ball, especially the slider, is not being overused and that it is being thrown correctly.

The Theory of the Breaking Ball

"Does the baseball really curve?" is a question that has created heated controversy ever since the curve became a part of the art of pitching shortly after the Civil War. William Arthur "Candy" Cummings, a five-foot nine-inch, 120-pound pitcher, is credited with mastering the first professional curveball, and he is enshrined in the Baseball Hall of Fame for his achievement.

But many scientists have disputed the reality of a curving baseball. In 1941, *Life* magazine commissioned strobe-light photographs of pitches and argued that a baseball did not curve (while its competitor, *Look*, took the opposite viewpoint). Hitters who have muttered to themselves after a strikeout about a ball that "rolled off a table" certainly don't believe that they fanned on an "optical illusion." And in the heat of battle with a pitch decision to make every few seconds, pitchers don't have the luxury of pondering the scientific mysteries of their devilish ally, the breaking ball. But before going to work on the mound, a pitcher can only help himself if he develops an intellectual understanding of how and why the breaking ball works. Good physical mechanics are vital to pitching success, but mental awareness can provide the extra dimension that separates pitchers from throwers.

In the previous chapter, I explained the theory of the rising fastball, a pitch that seems to defy gravity. When throwing your curveball, don't stress velocity, stress rotation. You are trying to maximize the spin and minimize the speed of the ball so that the batter sees more seam rotations and has his timing disrupted. A great hitter like Ted Williams was said to pick up a curveball's rotation only two feet out of a pitcher's hand. Fortunately for us practitioners of the craft, most hitters are not that talented, and the curveball remains a great asset.

Recent studies using high-speed photography and graphics computers have revealed exactly what happens to a well-thrown curveball. The magazine *Science 82* discovered that the arc on a curveball was established from the moment of release until its arrival in the catcher's glove. The movement of the curveball was largely downward with only a slight lateral movement; the slider's sideways movement at the hitting zone was greater. The curving force of the breaking ball was constant, but the pitch accelerated in the second half of its journey plateward because of an increase in gravitational force. The batter sensed greater movement, a "break" in the pitch, because he was standing sideways to the curving baseball. No wonder a well-rotated and well-placed breaking pitch can thoroughly befuddle a hitter.

Mastery of breaking pitches will not come easily, but it can be acquired with a lot of hard work. Although with practice you can improve control and consistency, and the movement and velocity of a fastball, it is principally a God-given asset. On the other hand, good curveball pitches and pitchers are made, not born.

Curveball Grips and Pressure Points

As with the fastball, the curveball grip and pressure points will depend on the individual pitcher. If you have mastered the art of keeping the ball hidden in your glove and maintain the

Pictured on the left is my main curveball, gripped with the four wide seams and well back in my hand. It is not choked, but the ball rests against the pad of my index finger beneath my knuckle. My thumb is on the side of the ball, just off contact with one of the narrow seams.

My alternate curveball grip, with the fingers along the two narrow seams, is pictured on the right. For both grips, my fingers are always on top of the ball and my wrist is turned to the side.

same hand position in the glove for all your pitches, you can hold the curveball virtually any way you desire.

My curveball is gripped like my fastball, across the two widest seams of the baseball, in order to get all four wide seams moving to the plate. But the curve is gripped using more of the finger surface than the fastball. I do not choke my curve—place it all the way back into my palm without any pressure from my fingertips—but I do have it resting against the pad of my index finger beneath my knuckle. The fleshy part of my thumb is on the side of the ball just off contact with one of the large seams.

Searching over the years for a consistent curveball—the kind that I could throw with more than an 85 percent chance that it would go where I wanted it—I have used many different pressure points. I used to throw my curve off my index finger, but in recent years, I find that the middle finger works better for me. You will only know what works best for your curve by trial and error in the bullpen and in the harsh reality of a ball game.

Curveball Release Points and Delivery

There is an absolute that must be remembered in releasing the curveball. You must throw the curve from top to bottom instead of from back to front. For a right-handed pitcher, "top to bottom" means releasing the ball from behind your right ear and following through to outside your left leg. (A left-handed pitcher's curve should be released from behind his left ear across to outside his right leg.)

The "back to front" motion is bad because you do not incorporate the whole body in the pitch; you simply throw it from the back of your head to the front of your head. You produce a curve that pitching coaches say is just "rolling" up to the plate with no sharp break. It has "looped" out of the hand upward, the downward plane has not been established, and thus you get no meaningful break on the ball.

To throw an effective curveball, remember the absolutes of pitching mechanics: (1) Keep your fingers on top of the ball. (2) Keep your elbow above your shoulder. (3) Get it out, get it up: Get the ball out of your glove and into throwing position as soon as you can.

If your fingers are on the side of the ball, the pitch will "hang" in a flat plane, and your day on the mound, if not your career, will be brief. If your elbow drops below your shoulder, your fingers will slip to the side of the ball and you will be short-arming the pitch from back to front.

I cock my wrist inward when I throw the curve. My *hand* is on the side of the ball while my fingers remain on top. The palm of my hand and the ball face my head. When I raise my throwing elbow, the shape of an "L" is made with my arm.

I rest my thumb on the bottom of the ball outside a seam, but, to repeat, thumb position varies greatly with each pitcher. Experiment with the thumb on or off a seam, taking careful note of the difference in pitch action. You want your curveball to go down and away sharply to a right-handed batter. Some days, that action occurs best with my thumb on a seam, other days with my thumb on a smooth portion of the ball. With experience, you will know what works best on a given day.

Whereas the fastball is released with backspin, the curveball is thrown with topspin; the rotation of the ball is toward the plate. As with the fastball, your elbow leads the way on the curveball and your forearm comes down afterward at a forty-five-degree angle. Your wrist in the curveball, however, is turned to the side.

Jim Palmer says that he almost can hear the ball snap as he releases his curve with his elbow in front of him. Carl Erskine, the standout Brooklyn Dodger hurler of the 1950's, imagined tickling his right ear upon release of his curve. Every pitcher will have a certain telltale feeling that indicates to him that he has thrown the curve correctly.

Don't imitate others. Work on developing an effective curve of your own, abiding by the absolutes of pitching mechanics and attempting to create the illusion that you are throwing a fastball. And keep your arm arc as wide as practicable.

Do not be discouraged if your curveball does not develop immediately. For some, it takes years to master the pitch. As I have said, I am still not satisfied with my curveball after seventeen seasons in the big leagues. I am still working to gain the confidence that I can throw my curve where I want to at least 85 percent of the time.

Youngsters can take solace from the careers of Sandy Koufax and Nolan Ryan. Koufax struggled for years before he developed the necessary control for his sensational curve. Fortunately, the Los Angeles Dodgers organization had the patience and intelligence to stick with him. Sandy said that before he mastered his curve, his pitching was like having a great camera but the film always turned out blank.

Sandy ultimately harnessed his great abilities. He combined his power and physical strength and suppleness (he had been a great basketball player) with his hard-earned insight into the art of pitching to become a Hall of Fame pitcher. On those days in his prime when Koufax had both his fastball and curve working, Ralph Kiner declared that he was guaranteed a three-hitter. He threw four no-hitters, and dominated the National League in the early 1960's.

The late St. Louis Cardinal third baseman and manager Ken Boyer once said that his teammate Bob Gibson, another Hall of Famer, was unbeatable, but Sandy Koufax was unhittable. Bothered throughout his career by an injured index finger, Koufax was strong enough to throw his curveball off his middle finger alone.

Nolan Ryan also required a long time to master a consistent curveball. The Mets lacked the Dodgers' patience and traded

Nolan to the California Angels, where he learned to control his curve. Combined with his awesome fastball, Nolan now had the stuff to throw five no-hitters, breaking Koufax's record, and dozens of low-hit masterpieces. Even more important than his records, Nolan has attained consistency and has continued to dominate hitters upon his return to the National League as a member of the Houston Astros.

The secret to Nolan's curveball is that he throws it with almost the same velocity as his fastball. When the ball breaks downward before the hitting zone, the hitter is almost helpless.

Nolan does not cock or "wrap" his wrist on his curveball. He uses a straight, relaxed wrist that has probably accounted for the durability of his arm. Many curveballers like me and Don Sutton simply cannot control the pitch with the straight wrist. As I have said many times, every pitcher will have to find the particular style that works best for him. Don't imitate Nolan Ryan's curveball if the grip and release don't fit your style. Do imitate the hard work and concentration that enabled Nolan to succeed after such a long struggle for mastery of the breaking ball.

Nolan Ryan grips his curveball across the wide seams of the baseball, but more off-center and farther back in his hand than for his fastball. His thumb pad makes firm contact with a bottom seam because Nolan applies substantial pressure to the bottom of the ball in throwing his outstanding curveball.

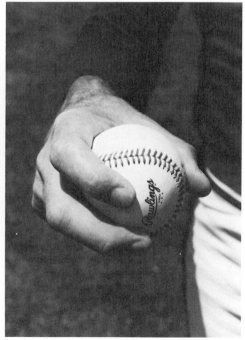

Curveball Target Points

You will also find many variations among successful curveballers in how they target their "jug," their "bender," their "yakker," their "Uncle Charlie," or their "yellowhammer"—just a few of the colorful names you will hear used to describe the curveball. Don Sutton, the master curveball specialist who has a genuine chance for three hundred career victories, keeps his head directly facing his catcher as he throws his curveball. So does Jerry Reuss, the fine southpaw of the Los Angeles Dodgers, who reminds himself to keep the ball low by telling himself, "Down with it! Down with it!" By turning his wrist slightly in or out, Jerry can change the movement on his curve while maintaining the same target. Starting from a slightly angled position on the mound, Nolan Ryan also keeps his head unvaryingly on his main target.

As for me, I cannot throw a good curve if I am aiming directly at my catcher: I wind up throwing wild-high or outside the strike zone. To compensate for my peculiarity, I instead pick up a preliminary target or focus point on my curve. It varies with the stuff I possess on a particular day. Normally, my focus point is the front hip, knee, or heel of the right-handed batter. For a left-handed hitter, I try to pick up the outside corner of the plate. If that is not working well on a given day, I look for the outside line on the batter's box only five inches above the ground.

Whatever targets you employ, keep in mind an absolute truth about throwing the curveball: *Aim for low in the strike zone.* Because the curveball is thrown with less velocity than the slider or fastball, your margin for error is greater. You don't have to be preoccupied with making it hit the corners of the plate, but avoid the high hanging curveball at all costs. A mediocre low curveball is far less likely to cause you trouble than a high hanger.

Keep in your head a mental picture of the purposes of a curveball: 1) to create the illusion in the batter's mind of a fastball coming in on the horizontal plane until, several feet from the plate, it falls downward in the vertical plane, and 2) a change of speed to break the hitter's timing.

As the stories of Koufax and Ryan demonstrate, curveball mastery does not happen overnight. I continue to struggle with mine. Practice and more practice is the only answer. Some

CURVEBALL

Areas of the curveball's effectiveness. When thrown low, the curve is effective the entire width of the plate, including down the middle. Note that the areas of effectiveness for the curve and the change are exactly the same (see page 132).

coaches recommend throwing darts to get used to the curveball motion. Johnny Sain, the former pitcher and current pitching coach, has developed a spinner—a baseball mounted on a little stand with a handle—to help pitchers understand how rotation and spin work. Sain encourages pitchers to practice their curveballs with this device by flipping up on the ball with their thumbs while pulling down on it with their index and middle fingers.

It is important to understand the principle of the spin on the curveball, but experience and practice on the mound are the best teachers. Under the tutelage of a knowledgeable coach, experiment with different grips and different pressure points. To reduce your velocity, work on shortening your stride slightly.

But don't overdo work on your curveball. The fastball is still the key to your success. Make sure you have the number-one pitch mastered before you fiddle around too much with the breaking ball. Putting the curve before the hummer is like putting the cart before the horse.

Slider Grips and Pressure Points

At its best, the slider utterly confounds the hitter who can never "sit" and wait on this pitch. The slider breaks too much to be a fastball but is thrown too hard to be a curve. Since it breaks late in the hitting zone, the batter rarely has time to react successfully to its sudden movement.

The slider is more of a power pitch than the off-speed curveball. It is usually easier to learn because of its greater velocity than the curve, but don't forget my earlier warnings about overusing the slider. It can cause physical damage to your elbow and arm and it can cause mental anguish when improperly thrown and "hung" in the hitting zone.

I grip my slider not quite as far back as the pad opposite my knuckle, as I do in the curveball, but not as close to the first joint as in the fastball. I use the index and middle fingers as my main gripping fingers.

As for the rising fastball and the curveball, I place my fingers across the two widest seams of the baseball in order to get all four wide seams rotating toward the plate. I place my thumb underneath, along a narrow seam. But unlike the riser, where I place my index and middle fingers in the middle of the wide

Steve Carlton uses basically the same grip for both his breaking pitches, the slider and the curveball. He grips them across two wide seams, so that all four seams will be biting the air. He holds both pitches out toward the fingertips of his index and middle fingers, which are less than a quarter inch apart, and he uses equal pressure on these fingertips. He applies more pressure with his thumb on a bottom seam.

The only difference between Steve's curve and slider is his angle of release. He throws his curve from over the top, near the twelve o'clock position of the dial, whereas his slider comes out more at forty-five degrees, at the two or two-thirty spot.

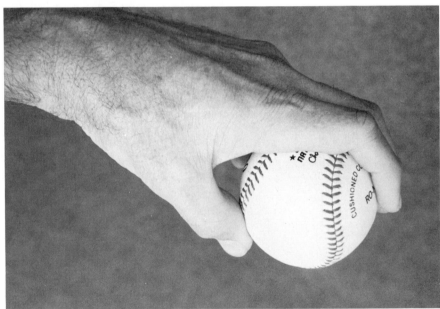

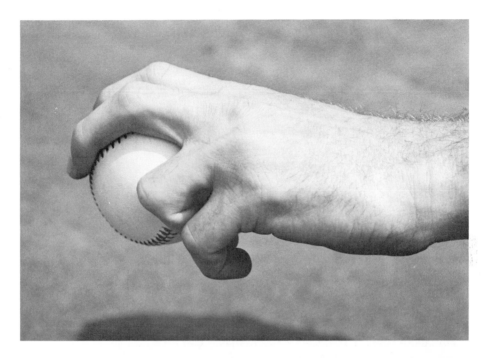

My slider grip is similar to the riding fastball (which you hope to deceive the batter into expecting), but I hold the slider farther back in my hand, approximately between the first and second joints of my index and middle fingers. I hold these fingers inside of a long seam instead of in the center, as I do for my fastball. I place my thumb underneath, along a narrow seam.

seams, for the slider I place my fingers along the inside of a long seam. I rotate the ball to the right during my delivery so the inside placement helps the movement in toward the batter.

This slight adjustment has provided handsome benefits for me. The batter, thinking fastball because of the tight rotation on the ball, cannot make the necessary adjustment when the ball breaks across and in or out on him. Remember that the meat of the baseball bat is eight inches at most. Throwing the pitch two inches farther out or one inch farther down from what the batter expects can make all the difference in the world. What might be a line drive or a home run now becomes a harmless groundout or a pop-up.

Slider Release Points and Delivery

Try to deliver your slider with proper mechanics. As I mentioned, this pitch jolts the elbow and can cause serious injury. Try to keep your wrist loose and flexible in the slider to take pressure off the elbow.

The release point on my slider is virtually identical to that on my fastball. I want my fingers to feel that they are on top of the ball, at the twelve o'clock position, but my arm comes toward the plate at about the ten or eleven o'clock position as seen from the batter's box.

The pressure point for my slider is the middle finger, not the index finger as it is for my fastball. Ferguson Jenkins and Jim Palmer use the middle fingers for their sliders, too, but, to repeat a vital point, if you know how to hide the baseball in your glove, you can use any pressure point without fear of giving away your pitches.

Jenkins says that upon release of his slider, his thumb points upward at the end of his follow-through. Palmer notes that his pressure fingers, index and middle, point toward home plate when he is done. Every pitcher has his personal guide to what feels right and what produces the best result. Just make sure that you are throwing the slider with the proper mechanics.

As in grips and pressure points, target points for your slider will vary widely. Tim McCarver, who caught Steve Carlton for many seasons with the Philadelphia Phillies, says that if he could see Steve's fingers directly on top of the ball from his crouch behind home plate, he knew that Carlton would be at the top of his game. For myself, as I have said about the curveball and fastball, I cannot target my slider successfully by looking directly at my catcher. Often I use the front hip of a batter as a focus point for my slider.

Like the curveball, the slider is most successful when thrown low in the strike zone. It is best thrown low and away to a right-handed hitter, but it can also be effective high and inside to a left-handed swinger.

There is also a "backdoor" slider that is a very effective pitch. You set up this pitch with a sinker out of the strike zone that appears to have the same type of rotation as a slider. When you throw the backdoor slider to a left-handed hitter, he thinks it is a sinker tailing outside of the strike zone and gives up on it. When thrown well, it breaks back over the plate for a called strike. The backdoor slider is an excellent pitch for a situation with a man on third and fewer than two outs, when you desperately need a strikeout.

There is also something that we call in the trade a "backup" slider. It is a mistake pitch that you can sometimes get away with, although most times, you won't. Your fingers slide off the top of the ball and go under it, and the pitch behaves like a sinking fastball. Instead of moving right to left, the backup slider "backs up" like a sinker and a batter can be fooled.

A backup slider is thrown even more incorrectly than a hanging slider and has even less velocity. I got my three-thousandth career strikeout on a backup slider against the Cardinals' Keith Hernandez, now my Met teammate. But it is a mistake pitch and don't fool yourself into thinking you can be a winning pitcher by violating one of the cardinal rules of pitching! Always keep your fingers on top of the ball. Remember another early lesson of this book: The higher up the ladder you rise in professional baseball, the more you will discover that hitters will take advantage of and crush your mistakes.

You need breaking pitches to become a complete pitcher. The curveball is harder to master than the slider, but is is well worth the effort, as proven by the outstanding careers Koufax and Ryan had once they mastered the pitch. The slider is easier to throw because the velocity is nearly as great as in the fastball. It, too, can help a good pitcher become a great one, as the careers of Ron Guidry and Steve Carlton prove. But don't overuse and abuse your breaking balls to the detriment of your number-one pitch, the fastball.

Understanding the primacy of the fastball and the complementary role of the breaking balls brings you to the threshold of mature pitching knowledge. But before you can say that you possess all the keys to the kingdom of pitching artistry, you must understand and utilize a pitch that I have grown to appreciate more with each passing season. Let us look at the theory and the practice of the change-up.

6 THE CHANGE-UP

Whoever first said that the art of pitching is the art of changing speeds deserves a place in the Hall of Fame. The sooner a high school phenom, who may have set all the strikeout records in the world, realizes this central fact about the art of pitching, the sooner he will move from the tenuous status of a thrower to an honored standing as a pitcher. Regardless of what sensational radar-gun readings you have amassed in high school or the low minor leagues, take my word that major-league hitters will ultimately catch up with your hummer if you don't have some off-speed pitches to confound their timing.

Nolan Ryan did not emerge as a dominant pitcher until he perfected his curve. While still thrown very hard, there was enough of a difference in speed to make a telling difference in the batter's response. Throughout recent baseball history, there have been many pitchers who made outstanding names for themselves by changing speeds artfully yet rarely throwing the ball more than eighty-five mph. The Yankees' Eddie Lopat, my former Cincinnati teammate Fred Norman, and today's American Leaguers Tommy John and Scott McGregor are just some of the many in this category.

I remember when Rod Dedeaux, my coach at the University of Southern California, took me into the bullpen to begin my instruction in the art of the change-up. He told me, "A change-up thrown at the knees is one hundred percent effective; a change-up thrown below the knees is fifty percent effective." I have found Coach Dedeaux's statement to be absolutely correct. If you maintain the arm speed of your fastball in throwing your change-up, there is no way that a batter can connect with your low change-up with any authority.

Low strikes, as I stressed earlier, are the key to effective pitching. To repeat, if you have thrown the batter's timing off with a change-up at the knees, you have successfully neutralized him. Even if you throw the change-up low and outside of the strike zone and the batter takes it for a ball, you have given him another speed to worry about. He turns up his dial at his peril now.

Mastering the change-up will take a lot of hard work and patience. Ray Sadecki, my former pitching teammate on the Mets, once told me that he doubted that I would ever be able to throw an effective change-up because I generated too much energy with every pitch. I am a very intense pitcher, who concentrates hard and sweats profusely on the mound. But I am proud that I have proved my friend wrong. In recent years, I have developed a change-up that I am not afraid to throw at any time in a ball game.

One of the great tactical advantages of throwing a change-up is that it can make your faster pitches that much more effective. If you establish a good change-up early in a game, you can conserve strength and stamina for the late innings. If your change is good enough, you may even be able to throw something less than your grade-A fastball past the hitters.

The earlier in your career you understand the importance of changing speeds on your pitches, the more successful and durable you will become. There are several kinds of change-ups, including the novelty pitches like Tug McGraw's screwball and Joe and Phil Niekro's knuckleballs. The principle of using the fastball to establish the off-speed pitch is the same in all these cases. I won't dwell on the specialty pitches, because they are highly unusual and were developed by particular individuals as a way to preserve their careers. The more common change-ups are the ones I will discuss in this chapter, the accelerated/decelerated fastball and the straight change.

In the early years of my career, I did not have a straight change-up but used at least three different speeds of fastball. The advantage of this strategy is that it assured that my fastball motion would be employed on all the pitches. The change-of-

CHANGE–UP

Areas of the change-up's effectiveness. As with the curveball, the change-up is effective the entire width of the plate, including down the middle. Don't forget that a well-executed change-up thrown low in the strike zone is a 100 percent effective pitch.

speed offering can be effective only if the entire delivery, from windup to release, is nearly identical to the fastball. The arm and hand speed must duplicate your fastball motion, and the arm and hand must come from the identical plane as your number-one pitch.

Nolan Ryan has been very successful using different speeds on his fastball as a means of changing pace. Imagine how the hitter must feel as he tries to turn his dial to connect with a ninety-two mile-per-hour fastball and then faces one above ninety-five mph. Nolan finds he has more success accelerating or decelerating fastballs in the high-nineties range than trying a straight change that may be more hittable in the mid-eighty mph range.

Most aspiring pitchers will not be endowed with Ryan's smoke, so I advise learning the straight change-up. As I have lost some velocity with the passage of time, this is the pitch I rely upon increasingly. The change-up is not a slowball, but an off-speed pitch thrown off your fastball.

Change-up Grips and Pressure Points

Even more than the other pitches, the change-up grip is the product of individual experiment and taste. Physique may dictate here as elsewhere. Tall, lean Jim Palmer grips the ball across the wide seams, as he does for all his pitches, and chokes the ball in the palm of his hand so that there is virtually no light visible between the thumb and his index finger. He uses his three middle fingers on top of the ball and feels pressure on his knuckles, not the fingertips, when he throws the change-up.

Another tall pitcher, Ferguson Jenkins, does not choke the ball but places it well back from the fingertips, using his cross-seam fastball grip. Don Drysdale, too, used to grip his change-up across the four wide seams to foster the illusion that his fastball was coming. Today, Mario Soto, the outstanding Cincinnati Red pitcher and my former teammate, grips the change-up similarly across the four wide seams.

I have tried the four-seam grip but usually find that I cannot control the change-up with it. I become wild-high that way, one of the worst plagues of a pitcher.

Through experimentation, I have come up with a grip similar to my sinker. I grip the ball near the two narrow seams, although I don't place my fingers directly on the seams but place

As in most change-ups, Nolan Ryan places the ball back in his palm, virtually choking it. The thumb rests on a seam with the index finger touching the bottom of the inside of the thumb. The pressure in throwing the change-up comes from the knuckles instead of the fingertips, which explains why the velocity of the change-up is slower than for the fastball.

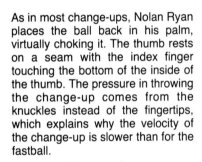

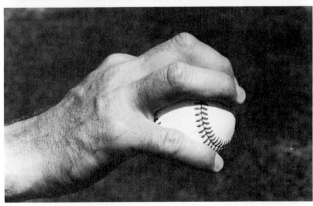

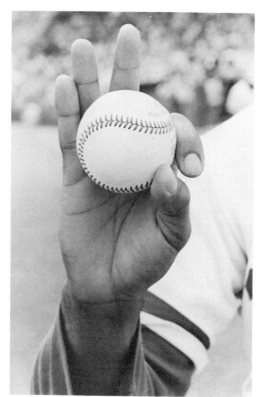

Mario Soto grips his outstanding change-up across the wide seams, with his index finger touching his thumb on the side of the ball. The ball is placed back toward the palm so the pressure in throwing the ball comes from the knuckles and not the fingertips.

I grip the ball for my change-up across the wide seams, but I remove my regular power finger, the index finger, from the ball by curling it off the ball into contact with the pad of my thumb. Without slowing my arm speed, I attempt to reduce the velocity of the ball by applying no pressure with my fingertips but only with my knuckles.

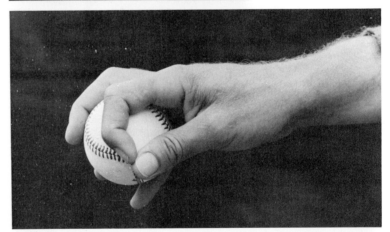

them slightly off-center. Unlike with my sinker, I don't use my index finger at all, but take it off the ball, bringing it in contact with my thumb. I feel that in taking my index finger, a key pressure finger in most of my pitches, off the ball, I have taken energy out of my delivery while maintaining my arm speed.

The change-up will require a lot of discipline and dedication to perfect, but if you work at it, you will experience the great joy of discovery. I remember the moment when I worked out my basic change-up grip. I was throwing in the outfield one day between starts with my teammate Jon Matlack of the Mets, and "Eureka!," after countless attempts, I found the grip that worked for me. In 1979, the Orioles' Mike Flanagan was throwing between starts with his teammate Scott McGregor and discovered that McGregor's change-up grip worked for him. Flanagan went on that year to win the American League Cy Young award.

Once you've found a successful change-up grip, don't think that you've learned it all. Keep experimenting with this pitch, because it can keep you potent for a long time. I even incorporated a four-seam change-up into my pitching arsenal at times during the 1983 season to give the batters something else to think about.

My main pressure point for the change-up is my middle finger. While my index finger is off the ball, my ring finger serves as a guide for the ball's journey plateward and also helps to reduce rotation on the ball. My thumb is tucked beneath the ball with the pad of the thumb tip resting atop a bottom seam. Mario Soto's thumb rests similarly, although the position of your thumb on most pitches will be subject to wide individual variation. Thumb position is not vital to the success of any pitch.

Change-up Release Points and Delivery

Keeping your motion nearly identical to your fastball motion is the hard part in mastering the change-up. I marvel at the ability of Ferguson Jenkins to deaden his right foot on the rubber as he delivers his change-up. Other pitchers find that increasing or shortening their stride to home plate serves the same purpose of taking energy out of the ball.

The key to throwing a successful change-up is to maintain the same motion, the same hand position, the same arm speed, and the same angle of delivery as for the fastball. A well-thrown change-up will look exactly the same to the hitter until it heads plateward and he is unable to adjust to its slower velocity. Compare my motion here to the fastball motion on page 62. In the fastball sequence, I am pitching from the stretch position rather than taking a full windup as I do here. The similarity between the two becomes obvious once I begin my kick.

I hide the change-up inside my glove, as I do on every pitch, and, for position and balance, try to maintain the feeling that the majority of my weight is on my right, pivot, foot (**A** through **G**). I start my knee lift, and rotate my hips, bringing energy into my motion. The knee also serves to block the batter's view of the ball (**H** through **N**). The ball does not become visible until **R** when I am well on the way to delivery of the baseball. My legs form a right angle as they land (**W** and **X**).

I cannot deaden my right leg or noticeably vary my stride on a change-up without thoroughly disrupting my pitching rhythm. What works for me is to goad myself mentally to achieve the desired result. I think, Fastball! Fastball! as I deliver the change-up. I try to maintain my normal arm speed while removing energy from the ball with my grip that excludes my power finger, the index finger.

I rock backward and start my motion, duplicating everything I would do in throwing the fastball. I keep my left side closed—knee, hip, and shoulder—until I am ready to release the ball. I remain compact in my motion and aim to drive my lower body toward the strike zone. I keep my elbow above my shoulder, establishing the basic forty-five-degree angle needed in throwing all the pitches.

The plane of release and the actual release of the ball should be as nearly identical to the fastball as possible. The wrist is flexible, but because the change-up is placed farther back in your hand than the fastball, you will feel more pressure at the knuckles than at the fingertips. The release motion on the change-up has been compared to that of pulling down a window shade. On a good change-up, the rotation will not be as great as on the fastball or the slider because you are not snapping it off.

Target Points for the Change-up

Remember that the change-up thrown at the knees is a 100 percent effective pitch, so you want your target point to be low. Don Drysdale used to goad himself to follow through with his wrist aimed at the dirt in front of home plate to keep his change-up low. For me, the target point is the catcher's feet. I have trouble keeping my pitches down if I aim higher.

Be careful that you don't tip off your change-up. If you drop your elbow and push the ball, the pitch will stay high and prove very appetizing for the batter. If you drop your elbow, the batter will know that a different kind of pitch is coming. Because it has significantly lower velocity, a poorly thrown high change-up is usually a source of much grief for a pitcher.

The secret to a successful change-up is to maintain your normal arm speed until the last fractional moment of release. When properly delivered, the change-up is a marvelous pitch because the reduction in speed and the location low in the strike zone keep the batter thoroughly bottled up. It may take years to master, but that's why a young pitcher should start early in his career to work on an effective change.

Other Kinds of Change-ups

There are other variations on the change-up such as the forkball, the palmball, and the slip pitch. They take less out of your arm than the screwball because the wrist is not snapped during delivery. I cannot overstress how important the wrist is to a pitcher. As a very pliable part of the arm, it should be kept flexible on virtually all your pitches except if you are throwing that rare novelty pitch the knuckleball, which utilizes a stiff wrist. The following pitches, while difficult to master, are useful because they do not cause much physical strain when thrown with the proper mechanics.

The forkball requires a large hand because you place the ball between the index and middle fingers of your throwing hand. The ball slides from between these two fingers with little wrist action and usually goes down. But it requires great skill to master it for strikes.

The palmball is placed deep in the hand with all the fingers gently curved around the ball. The pressure point usually is applied off the inside joint of the thumb.

The slip pitch is a variant of the palmball in which the ball is choked deep in the palm and slips out between the thumb and one of the fingers. Mickey Lolich used to throw an effective slip pitch. As I noted earlier, Lolich was one of the few pitchers I know who threw all his pitches without utilizing any seams.

I repeat, however, that the aspiring pitcher is best advised to try to master the basic change-up. You should also adopt early on the philosophy of changing speeds on your fastball and other pitches. Intellectually, the use of a good change-up will broaden your knowledge of and perspective on the art of pitching. There is a special joy in fooling the batter with a change-up. A basic rule of pitching is, "Keep the batter off-stride," and the change-up serves that end perfectly.

The off-speed pitch also conserves your arm. Because it is delivered with a flexible wrist, no pitcher ever developed arm trouble throwing the change-up. The slider, on the other hand, can put tremendous stress on the elbow, which explains why so many pitching coaches and organizations are wary of throwing that pitch too often.

As you gain experience pitching, you should be able to throw the change-up in virtually any situation. An aggressive hitter who is dying for a fastball—you can see that like a big neon sign!—is a perfect candidate for a change-up or even a diet of change-ups. Once you have mastered this pitch, you will be able to succeed on those days when you do not have your best velocity, location, or movement on your fastball. With time, you should be able to develop off-speed variations on your curveball and other breaking pitches.

The change-up is not a "slowball," but a pitch thrown off a fastball from which you have decreased the velocity. Thrown consistently at or below the knees, the change-up will keep the batter off-stride and unable to hit the ball with any regularity.

A strong young pitcher may resist learning the change-up. He takes pride in muscling the ball past the hitter, but forgets that changing speeds can thwart the batter just as easily and with less physical wear on the arm. The further you progress in the game of baseball, the greater the likelihood that hitters will occasionally nail your fastball and even your slider. Spare yourself unnecessary hard times and work on the change-of-speed pitch. It will give the batter something extra to think about and will conserve your arm for those times when your only option is to try to throw the ball past him.

7 THE FIFTH INFIELDER: HELPING YOUR DEFENSE

I agree wholeheartedly with the old axiom "Baseball is a game won on pitching and defense." A good fielding pitcher can help his own cause immeasurably. Except for those special situations in which a pitcher needs a strikeout to insure that base runners don't advance, good pitching strategy is premised on making the batter hit the ball to one of your fielders. Once the delivery is complete and the ball released, the pitcher becomes the fifth infielder. No pitcher, no matter how talented, can consider his education complete without understanding the principles and practices of fielding his position.

The first and most crucial principle is self-defense. Your glove should always be up, in front of your body, poised to protect your face and body and ready to snare any ground ball or line drive. You may have thrown the ball to home plate at ninety miles per hour, but as the old saying goes, "It came back at a hundred fifty miles per hour." That should be warning enough that you are the closest fielder to the hitter and have precious little time to react to the ball.

Compounding your vulnerability is the fact that you don't normally maintain the complete body balance that your infielders can. As a result, your reactions must necessarily concentrate on self-defense. Photographs of Herb Score of the Cleveland Indians being struck by the batted ball of Gill McDougald of the Yankees in 1957—an incident that curtailed Score's potentially great career—should be enough of a lesson to any young pitcher.

As always in the game of baseball, the specific situation will determine your reactions. For instance, if there are no runners

Throwing to first base. Always remember that when the ball is hit or bunted to you, you must follow basic infielding techniques. Bend down to keep the ball in front of you and scoop it up with both hands. Straighten up and take the infielder's basic crowhop (step and a half) in the direction of first base. Make a firm, accurate throw to the base.

Throwing to third base. You can really help your cause if you have mastered the footwork necessary to nail a runner trying to move to third base on a bunt. Get off the mound quickly and step across the path of the ball with your right foot. Plant your left foot as you bend down to pick up the ball. Turn toward third base and make a quick but accurate toss. You don't have the luxury of taking a crowhop when throwing to third base, which is why a lot of time is spent in spring training on mastering this footwork.

on base, the pitcher does not have to catch every ball hit back to him. It is sometimes very difficult to judge correctly how hard the ball is hit. Your body is still in motion as you follow through and the speed of the ball coming off the bat may be difficult to gauge.

With no runners on base, simply stop the ball. Knock it down with an open glove, retrieve it, and make a sure throw to first base. You should have enough time to nail the runner. Sometimes if you close your glove on the ball too quickly, you can lose the entire play. The technique of knocking the ball down and then throwing it usually works with a runner on second, too. Once you retrieve the ball, you eye the runner, hold him to his base, and throw to first.

With runners on first or third or in multiple-runner situations, you don't have the luxury of simply knocking the ball down. In these situations, you must try for a clean catch, and depending on what your catcher shouts at you and your knowledge of the baserunners' speed, you must close the glove, reach for the ball, initiate the appropriate footwork, and make an accurate throw to the chosen base.

Throwing to the Bases

In throwing to the bases, accuracy is more important than speed. If you rush your throw trying to start a double play, you may lose both outs. I find that gripping the ball across the seams results in a straight, accurate toss. But sometimes you do not have the chance to choose a preferred grip if you are trying to nail a runner with sprinter's speed.

It is imperative that you make the throw chest high so that your fielder can get out of the way of base runners sliding in spikes high, especially at second base. In throwing the ball chest high, you give your infielder greater range in which to catch the ball, increasing your margin for error on a wide or errant throw. Many middle infielders' careers have ended abruptly because a teammate, perhaps a pitcher, fired a low throw that left them at the mercy of an oncoming runner. You will earn your infielders' silent but genuine gratitude by delivering the ball chest high, thereby protecting their ankles from the slide of the base runner.

The proper mechanics of throwing to an infielder are similar to those of pitching to a catcher.

Point your lead toe directly at your target, just as you should do in delivering the ball to home plate. Try to keep your fingers on top of the ball and throw overhand to give your fielder a straight throw to handle. You don't want to throw balls that sail or sink. The straighter and more accurate your throws, the easier it will be for him to make his play, either a tag of a runner or a bag or the relay on the double play.

When throwing to second on the double play, you should know where your infielders want to receive the ball from you. As a general rule, never throw directly on the bag to your middle infielder. He will want to catch the ball in mid-stride, step on the bag, and pivot off it in one fluid motion to complete the relay to first. With the shortstop covering, you should aim your throw one step to the left-field side of the bag; if the second baseman covers, aim your throw one step to the right-field side of the second-base bag.

Always make sure that you are balanced before throwing the ball. Take the infielder's basic crowhop, the step-and-a-half shuffle in the direction where the throw is going, and make an accurate toss.

Covering First Base

On any ball hit to the right side of the infield, it is the pitcher's responsibility to break to cover the first-base bag. Make it second nature to break toward first even on line drives to first or second. There is no guarantee that the line drive will be caught, and an alert pitcher can prevent the loss of a sure out by being ready to make the putout at first.

A good, aggressive catcher will always goad you with reminders, "Get over there! Get over there!" Don't wait for an invitation. It's your job to cover the bag and receive throws from the first baseman or, if the ball has eluded him, from the second baseman.

When well executed, the pitcher-covering-first play is one of the most geometrical plays in baseball. It embodies all the aspects of teamwork so important to good baseball defense. Run to first base on a diagonal path from the mound until you are about eight to ten feet from the bag and parallel to the first-base foul line. Do not run directly to the base, because if there is a bad throw toward the infield, you will find it hard to reach back and catch it.

Throwing to second base. Make sure beforehand you know who is covering second, the shortstop or the second baseman. Step across the path of the ball with your right foot. Reach down and keep the ball in front of you while moving your body in a line toward second. Take the crowhop toward second and make an accurate toss chest high and on the shortstop side of the bag to keep your infielder from a collision with the onrushing base runner.

Covering first base. The moment *any* ball is hit to the right side, a pitcher must break for first base. You head diagonally toward the base until you reach the edge of the infield grass, about eight to ten feet from first base. If the fielder is throwing to you for the putout, you use your glove as a high target for him. In two steps, you should be able to tag the outside corner of the bag with the right side of your right foot. Once you tag the base, immediately whirl around to get into throwing position in case other base runners are trying to advance.

The fielder should try to hit you with a good throw chest high. Keep your glove raised to chest level to provide a good target. The principle of your own throws to second holds true for the first (or second) baseman's throw to you with the exception that the right-side fielder should try to get you the ball two steps from the bag. In so doing, you can catch the ball and in your first step find the exact location of the bag. In your second step, you can tag the bag and make the out.

Of course, sometimes you won't have the luxury of that much time. You will have to take the throw from your infielder and tag the first-base bag all in one motion. With practice, you can acquire this defensive skill, getting the feeling of how many steps it takes to get to the bag and touch it with the right foot. Eventually, you should be able to reach and tag the bag without ever looking at the base.

I recommend that you catch the ball with your gloved hand alone instead of with two hands. You are getting a lob toss from your fielder, so you should be able to handle the throw easily with just your glove. Your throwing hand will then be free to provide better body balance for any throws you may have to make after the putout.

I also advise tagging the bag with your right foot (this applies to both left-handed and right-handed pitchers). You want to keep your body out of the way of the base runner to avoid collision and a possible interference call. With your right foot touching the bag and your right hand free to guide you to turn back toward the other bases, you are in good position to make any other throws.

Be especially vigilant when the opposing team has a runner on second with fewer than two outs. When you run to cover first, the man on second may try to catch you sleeping and score while you have your back turned to him. If you follow the proper mechanics of covering first base—catching with the gloved hand and tagging the bag with your right foot—you will be ready to thwart any reckless ambitions of the runner.

Backing Up the Bases

Inevitably in the game of baseball, a batter will drive one of your pitches for extra bases. As always, you must be mentally prepared for all possible situations.

For instance, if a man is on first and the ball is clearly heading into an outfield gap for extra bases, you must be ready to either back up the catcher at home plate or back up third base. You must get into a position near the third-base line that will allow you to see the play developing and to gauge where your defense is going to throw the ball.

As in pitch selection, backing up bases requires decisions based on many factors. How hard was the ball hit? What is the speed of your outfielders and the base runners? Are you playing on speedy artificial surface or slower grass? Does the score of the game dictate cautious or adventurous baserunning by your opponent? It is your job to know the situation and to make your backup decision based on an intelligent reading of all the factors. You never know when an alert play of yours—grabbing an overthrow and nailing an advancing runner—will get you out of a tough inning and save you a ball game.

The prerequisite for making a good defensive play is to be thinking like a fielder the moment your pitch is released. You do neither yourself nor your team any good by fretting about the mistake that caused the hard-hit ball. It may not even have been a mistake, but just a major-league hitter doing what he is paid to do. As I mentioned earlier, a pitcher must accept this humbling fact of life: Despite your best efforts, good hitters will sometimes clout the best of pitches.

Do not mope after an extra base hit has been tagged off you. And, especially, do not point fingers at your teammates for errors they have made that have put you in a jam. During the long season and even within the cycles of individual games, there will be times when your fielders bail you out of your pitching mistakes by making great plays. You are all in the field together; you live or you die together. That is the proper attitude for the professional pitcher to carry out to his business on the mound.

Pick-off Plays and Keeping Base Runners Close at First Base

One of the best methods of defusing an opponent's baserunning skills is to have the ability as a pitcher to keep the runners close to the first-base bag. If it doesn't distract you from your main business at hand, which is always the man on the plate, a good pick-off move to first can help your defensive play considerably.

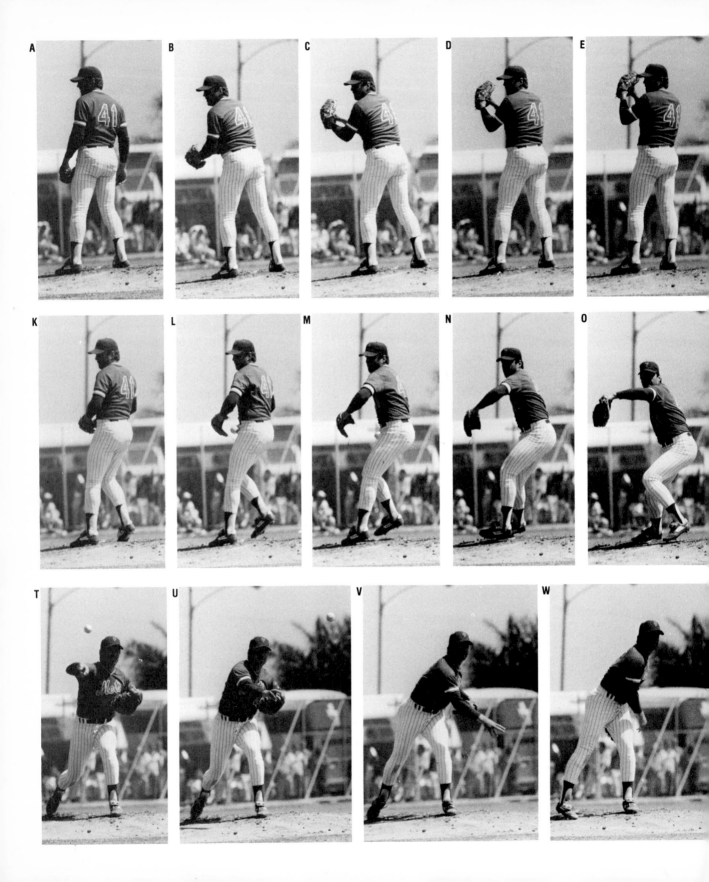

G

H

I

J

Q

R

S

The key to a good pick-off motion is quick feet. You start the motion by assuming a normal stretch position. The right side of your right foot is in contact with the rubber, with your left foot parallel to it and about a half stride forward. Bring your hands to the normal set position, as if you were going to pitch to home plate, but instead of throwing home, you rise on the left side of your right foot and pivot toward first base with the ball of your left foot. The throw should not be lobbed; it should be quick and accurate. You don't want to make it wild, enabling the runner to gain an extra base. Even if you don't pick the runner off, you have at least let him know that you might come back there again and may thus shorten his lead.

I must confess that I have never had a good pick-off motion. You need quick, almost dancing feet, such as those exhibited by Atlanta Braves' veteran knuckleballer Phil Niekro, and I have not been endowed with that quickness. I also have a relatively high knee lift that runners can take liberties with.

I have been fortunate in my career to have worked with fine defensive catchers—Jerry Grote, Johnny Bench, Mike O'Berry—whose strong throwing arms have often offset my mediocre ability to hold runners close. Not pleased with my shortcoming in this area, I continue to try to improve my motion to first base.

Inspired by the mirrors I saw in the clubhouses of Japanese baseball teams, I work on my pick-off move in front of a mirror at home or in the trainer's room at the ball park. I recommend dissecting your motion in front of a mirror to see how your body operates on your pick-off move. You may see by some telltale movement of hand or leg that you are giving a base runner and his coaches an important edge. You may notice that you invariably throw to the plate or to the base using two different positions.

Mixing up your throwing pattern, both to the base and to the plate, is also good strategy. Throw gently to your first baseman, then throw hard. Keep in mind that if you are not standing on the rubber, you can bluff a throw to first without a balk being called. You never know when you may catch an unsuspecting base runner off-guard.

When delivering the ball to the batter, mix up your pattern as well, quick one time, holding the ball longer in your stretch, thereby freezing the runner the next time. Remember the two basic rules in keeping a runner honest: (1) Don't let him take a walking lead, which means that you must make him stop before you release the ball to the plate. If he has built up a head of steam before you even throw the ball, he is almost guaranteed to steal a base. (2) Establish a point in your mind at which you will not let the runner advance in his lead. If he goes past that point, throw to first, driving him back to the bag.

The best pick-off throw to first is a quick wrist flip aimed below your first baseman's knee and to the inside of the bag, so he can apply a quick tag. If you are a power pitcher, don't make the mistake of thinking your throws to first should have extra mustard on them. Quite the contrary. Make them crisp and low, easily handleable by your first baseman.

Avoiding the Balk

Section 8.05 of the Official Baseball Rule Book spells out many of the no-no's that result in a balk—a penalty against the pitcher that gives all base runners the gift of an extra base. The commonest balk violation occurs with a runner on first base. In an attempt to confuse the base runner, the pitcher does not come to a full stop in his stretch position on the mound before either throwing to the base or beginning his motion toward the plate. Good base runners can rattle a pitcher and cause him to lose his composure. He may then start making unnatural movements on the mound, thus alerting the umpires to balk possibilities.

The best way to avoid balking is to learn a comfortable stretch position and to realize that with men on base, nobody can hold a gun to your head and order you to throw the ball. (Technically, the rule book requires a pitcher to throw the ball within twenty seconds if there are no men on base.) You can always step off the rubber and drive the runner back to first base in that way.

We wisely spend a lot of time in spring training trying to master the mechanics of the pick-off motion. It involves turning off the rubber with the right foot, planting the left foot toward first base, and making the quick throw to first. (Left-handers can, of course, see first base more easily, but they should never become so predictable and casual toward the runner that they give him an edge.)

If, in spite of all your efforts at keeping him close, you sense that the runner is about to steal anyway, give your catcher a good ball to handle at home plate. Try to throw it chest high, but slightly out of the strike zone where the hitter cannot get to it.

Pick-off Plays at Second Base

Picking off a runner in scoring position at second base can greatly aid your cause, but you must have perfect coordination with your infielders. Signs and acknowledgments of signs are necessary for making the pick-off at second work. A sign may be the touching of a cap or the calling of your name by the shortstop or second baseman, and your acknowledgment may be the touching of your cap or the back of your neck.

The so-called daylight play, used to pick off a base runner taking too liberal a lead at second base, is one of the prettiest plays in the sport. It is used when the pitcher glances toward second base and finds that the shortstop has edged toward the bag behind the base runner, leaving daylight between himself and the unsuspecting runner. On a prearranged signal or through eye contact made when they spotted the straying runner, the pitcher and the shortstop start silently counting, one, two, three, as the pitcher turns his head back toward home plate. On two, the shortstop breaks toward second as the pitcher whirls around, nearly 360 degrees, and on the count of three delivers the ball low on the bag to the shortstop. Sometimes you will see a pitcher step directly toward second and throw instead of whirling, but the runner has more time to react to this throw because the pitcher cannot get as much on the ball as he does by whirling.

Remember that you cannot balk to second base. Even if you cannot pull off the precise timing required for the daylight play, you can always bluff the runner back to second. Remind him that you know he is there. Keeping him close to the bag will give your outfielders a better chance of throwing him out at the plate on a single.

Pick-off plays at third base are very rare because the third baseman does not hold a runner on the bag. If you are concerned about a possible steal of home, pitch from a stretch. If you decide to make a pick-off throw to third, the movement is simple. You stop, step, and throw. You may decide that the risk of throwing the ball into left field is too great. Remember that to keep the runner close, all you need to do is step off the rubber.

To sum up the principles of pick-offs, it is always a good idea to remind runners on any base that you are aware of them and their potential threat. Cat-and-mouse games to keep them cautious are good tactics. But never allow base runners to deflect you from the main purpose of your craft, retiring the batters at the plate.

Fielding Plays: Bunts and Pop-ups

The bunt situation arises frequently, especially in the National League, where the pitchers still hit for themselves. The ideal method of thwarting a bunt is to stop the batter from laying down a successful one. Two of the best pitches to prevent a sacrifice bunt are high fastballs and sharp sliders away. If you think a squeeze play may be coming, aim your pitch at the right-handed batter's shoulder to move him out of the batter's box. Your catcher should then have room to make a tag on the sliding runner.

If the bunt is laid down in fair territory, the best way to determine which base to throw to is to use the number system: "one" for first base, "two" for second, "three" for third, and "four" for home. The simpler the communication among you, your catcher, and your infielders, the easier it will be to make the play quickly. As you advance up the ladder of professional baseball and play before progressively larger crowds, the noise level will become a disruptive factor. At the discretion of your manager, of course, keep your signals simple.

If you field a bunt, the catcher should call out the number of the base for you to throw to. Make sure you turn and plant your feet and balance yourself, as in all your throws, before throwing. Take the basic crowhop before releasing the ball.

If you are throwing to first and the base runner hustling down the line is blocking your view, aim your throw slightly to the infield side of the foul line. You don't want to contribute to a potential big inning by hitting the runner with the ball.

If a bunt is popped up high, you must call out the position of the infielder who has the best chance of catching it. A weakly popped-up bunt may be best caught by you coming off the mound. But don't forget that on any pop-up, bunt or not, it is your responsibility to make the call for your defense. Do not call too early, but try to judge who has the best angle on the ball and who seems to be most on-balance. Then call that infielder's position loud enough for the whole infield to hear. The ideal time to make your call is when the ball reaches the peak of its arc.

Tag Plays

When called on to make a tag, follow basic infielder techniques. If a runner is coming in standing up, tag him with both hands, the ball securely in the glove, the free hand securely around the ball. If the runner is sliding, keep your pitching hand out of the way of his approaching spikes. Tag him with your glove, keeping the glove between the base and the runner. Make a quick tag and get the ball and the glove out of there as quickly as possible.

Playing Pepper

What a wonderful and useful little game pepper is! Pitchers should play it regularly from spring training until the end of the season. With one man batting and no more than three fielders lined up closely together, you will find that your reflexes, the basic eye-hand coordination so central to baseball skill, will improve dramatically.

A crisp game of pepper can exhaust even a well-conditioned pitcher in twenty minutes. The batter stands twenty to thirty feet away from the fielders and as they lob the ball to him he swings away, hitting hard grounders or line drives. The ball may take a bad hop, causing you to suffer what we call "shin-burgers," but better that you get toughened to your fielding craft in a game of pepper than in the heat of battle in a real game.

Pepper is a great teacher of self-protection, the most fundamental principle of fielding for a pitcher. In a fun situation, pepper recreates all the plays you will have to face when the game is on the line. Make a little game out of it among your teammates, seeing how many grounders or liners you can grab without making a boot. Regularly switch off from the fielding line to the batting position in pepper. I assure you that a daily dose of pepper will provide preventive relief from the defensive lapses that can cost you ball games.

Signs with Your Catcher

Clear and efficient communication with your catcher is obviously beneficial. A pitcher should have the confidence to call his own game, but a catcher who knows you well and understands how you want to pitch different kinds of hitters can be a tremendous asset in the art of pitching. Signals between pitchers and catchers will vary from team to team and sometimes from pitcher to pitcher. The important thing is to establish communication with your catcher before the game and stick to a system. When in doubt, you can always call time and confer with your receiver.

The commonest set of pitch signals is the number system: one for fastball, two for a curve, three for a slider, and four for a change-up. Just as you should vary your pick-off motion, so should you mix up your rhythm in receiving pitch signals. Remember the hitter sees and registers in his computer everything you do on the mound. Do not allow yourself to settle into recognizable patterns.

Ferguson Jenkins once said that the pitcher and the catcher are called the battery because they put the charge into any game. They can also short-circuit it if they are not alert to sign stealing. Willie Mays can credit dozens of his home runs as a San Francisco Giant to the brilliant sign stealing of his first-base coach, Wes Westrum. When on the mound you must be careful not to give away either your pitch grips or the signs from your catcher.

I remember once pitching to Joe Morgan during his glory years with the Reds before I became his teammate. Joe saw me give a circular signal to my catcher, indicating that I wanted to run through the signs again. When I quickly nodded, Joe assumed that the ol' number one, the fastball, was coming. He stood there in amazement as a slow curve broke over the plate. "Whaddaya doin', man?" Joe complained, realizing that he had been fooled.

When a runner is on second base, he looks directly into the catcher's crouch and poses a sign-stealing danger. So before the game you must work out a different series of signs with your catcher. There are generally two kinds of signs with the runner on second, indicator signs and pump signs.

The indicator sign is a number that the catcher puts down *after* which the next number is the pitch he is calling for. For example, if you have arranged that "two" is your indicator and the catcher puts down three-one-two-three, the pitch is "three," the slider, the number that came after the indicator "two."

With pumps, the key is the number of pumps the catcher makes with his fingers after he gives you the key number. If it is "two" again, and the catcher puts down one-two-three-three-one, for example, the pitch is again the slider because it is three pumps after the key. The number is just a camouflage. You also can shake off the signs with the runner on second, having a prearranged second key number. A fastball in this situation may be indicated by the number five because you have run through

Signals between pitchers and catchers will vary from team to team and sometimes from pitcher to pitcher. The important thing is to establish communication with your catcher before the game and stick to a system. When in doubt, you can always call time and confer with your receiver.

I am calling for a slider by putting down three fingers.

One finger pointed to the right leg indicates the pitcher wants a fastball into a left-handed hitter.

I am putting down four fingers, which usually indicates a change-up. Sometimes, just wiggling all the fingers indicates a change-up.

The fist indicates the sign for a pitch-out.

One finger is the standard sign for the fastball.

Two fingers is the usual sign for the curveball.

One finger pointed toward the left leg indicates the pitcher wants a fastball into a right-handed hitter.

the basic four pitches without deciding on the pitch to throw.

Whatever method you choose, make sure that you can see the catcher's signals clearly. Some pitchers have asked their backstops to put a little white tape on their fingers so they are sure that they are picking up the signs correctly.

When you gain experience working with a catcher, there will be a wonderful feeling of teamwork between you, two heads thinking as one. Many times, when you see a pitcher shake off a sign from a catcher, it is not out of disagreement but to throw doubt into the batter's mind just before the release of the ball. Remember that everything you do on the mound registers in the batter's mind. A little camouflage in close communication with your catcher can sometimes provide you with the winning edge.

My final recommendation for helping your defense is one of the most important: *Work quickly.* You may need a little more time between pitches with men on base in a tight situation, but there is no excuse for dawdling with no men on. A pitcher who works fast almost always receives better defensive support from his teammates than a hurler who seems to take forever between pitches. It stands to reason that the fielders' concentration will wander if you procrastinate on the mound, wondering and worrying about the next pitch.

A crisply working pitcher keeps his fielders on their toes because they know that the ball may be hit to them at any time. A fast pace and good control mean that the hitters usually go after the first and second pitches offered. The tempo of the game speeds up and, necessarily, your defense remains "in" the game. The bottom line is that the fast-working pitcher reaps the greatest benefit from his teammates' defensive alertness.

THE MAINTENANCE OF PITCHING FITNESS

The game is over and you have given your all in a starting assignment. Regardless of the outcome—whether you've lost a squeaker, won a laugher, or had a no-decision in a game lost by errors—you accept the result. If you're a big leaguer, there are 162 games and you cannot afford to get either too high after a win or too low after a loss. Your job physically is to restore your fitness and pitching by the day of your next start. You have torn your body down during the game. Now, slowly and patiently, you must build your strength back up.

You probably have seen photos of pitchers in the clubhouse after a game, icing down their pitching shoulder with an ice bag tied to the arm by an ace bandage. Sandy Koufax may have been the first hurler to popularize soaking his arm, especially his arthritic elbow, in ice. Because success spawns imitation, wits have said that if Koufax had soaked his arm in oats, pitching hopefuls would have made a beeline to the stables.

Ice does serve a very important therapeautic purpose. It reduces the swelling inevitably caused by the severe toll pitching takes on your arm and shoulder. Ice also eases the micro-tears in your blood vessels that arise during the sustained throwing of a baseball.

Having iced yourself down for about twenty minutes, you can return home for, one hopes, a good night's sleep. I recommend leaving the emotions from the game's outcome in the clubhouse. There will be plenty of time in the days ahead to assess what you've learned about your opponents and yourself in the game just completed.

If you wake up the next morning a little stiff in the lower back and legs, there is nothing to worry about. What you must guard against is continued soreness in your body. Continuing pain indicates a serious problem and you should consult a physician before exercising to rebuild your strength. As you gain experience in pitching, you will be able to distinguish between minor stiffness and potentially serious soreness. I explain the difference by saying that stiffness can be worked out of the arm with increased blood flow, but soreness will not work itself out and exercise simply continues to aggravate the muslces in question.

When you arrive at the ball park the day after you started a game, you have a busy regimen ahead of you. In the major leagues, and increasingly in the minor leagues as well as the good college programs, expert trainers are available to help us work out the kinks from yesterday's performance and to prepare us for our next start. The extent of the trainer's resistance work with you will depend on how much you threw the day before, how long before your next start, and how good your general condition is. But unless you are very tired during a particularly

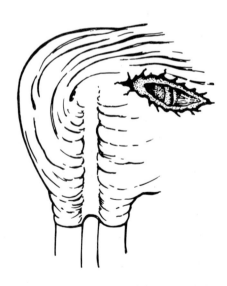

LONGITUDINAL CUFF TEAR,
SUPRASPINATUS (as viewed from back)

This drawing shows the dreaded rotator-cuff tear in the supraspinatus muscle. In most cases of this injury, improper pitching mechanics have caused the delicate shoulder to bear too much of the burden of pitching stress. If the cuff is torn, extended rest is usually the first prescription. If that fails, surgery, with no guarantee of success, is the only answer.

steamy part of the summer, I strongly recommend doing these exercises with special care and intensity the day after you pitch. Your rotator cuff is stiffest on this day, and the lactic acid throughout your body needs to be removed through exercise.

Lactic acid is carried in the bloodstream and accumulates in the muscles during periods of strenuous activity when the body cannot fully keep up with the muscles' demand for oxygen. At one level this process results in the minor muscle soreness and stiffness experienced by weekend athletes. But if too much lactic acid enters the muscles, they will cramp and ultimately be unable to move at all. A well-conditioned professional athlete can still compete—his muscles will still contract—with considerable amounts of lactic acid in his system. However, the sooner the lactic acid is converted through stretching and exercise into carbon dioxide and water and exhaled through the lungs, the healthier the athlete will be. A major purpose of the small-weight work and the trainer-assisted exercises is to free your body of unwanted substances like lactic acid.

Isometric and Isokinetic Exercises

I do both isometric and isokinetic resistance exercises. Isometric work involves resistance against an immovable object, constant effort against the resistance supplied by the trainer. Isokinetic exercises involve variable resistance supplied by the trainer depending on a pitcher's strength throughout the whole range of motion.

The goal of the isometric and isokinetic exercises is exactly the same as the goal of the small-weight work. You are trying to build up equal strength in all the muscles of the rotator cuff. The procedure is identical in both. You are trying to recreate through physical drill the motion of pitching. You want to work out the kinks and increase the flexibility as well as the strength of the entire rotator-cuff aggregate, the external and internal rotator muscles and the supraspinatus and infraspinatus muscles. You also want to exercise and stretch the numerous other muscles of the shoulder and the arm.

I do the isometric and isokinetic work on the trainer's table. As in the weight work, you begin these manually assistive exercises with a warm-up to stimulate the blood flow into the

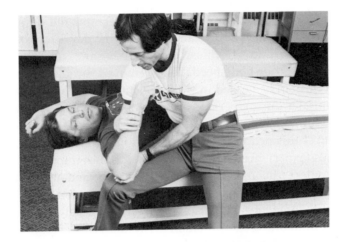

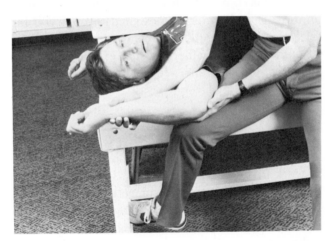

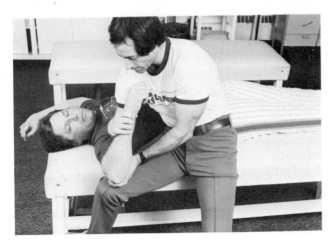

Exercise 1. I begin my external rotation warm-up lying on my back with Larry sitting on the table by my right side. Larry's right hand is on my right wrist and his left hand stabilizes my elbow. Larry applies slight pressure and I move my arm back against his resistance, pause, and return to the starting position. We do this warm-up five to ten times.

Exercise 2. The internal rotation warm-up is similar to the external rotation warm-up but the direction of movement is reversed. Begin with the arm in the downward position, raise the arm against slight pressure applied by the trainer, pause, and return to the starting position. I repeat this warm-up fewer than ten times since my internal rotators are already very strong from the forward motion of pitching.

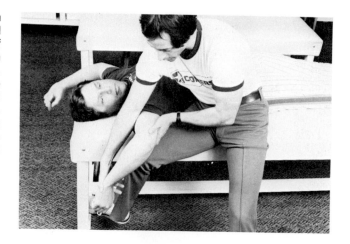

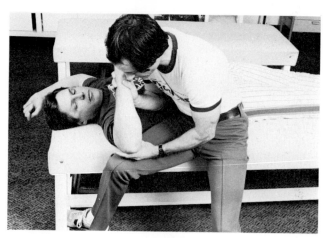

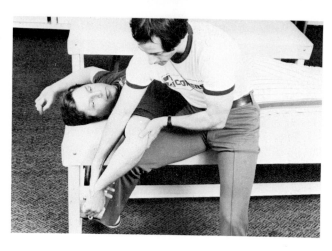

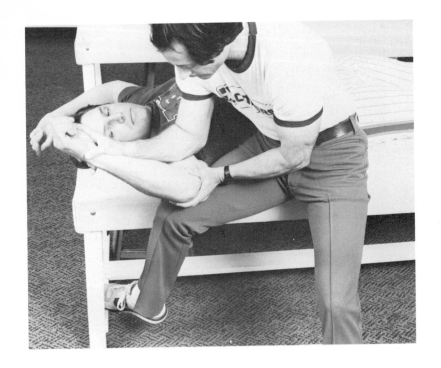

Exercise 3. The external rotation stretch is similar to the external rotation warm-up. Larry grasps my right elbow firmly with his left hand and holds the inside of my right wrist with his right hand. He takes my arm back as far as possible without pain or discomfort and holds me there for between five and eight seconds. The stretch is repeated between five and seven times. Remember that every pitcher's strength and flexibility will be unique, so don't be surprised or disappointed if you don't achieve at the outset the kind of limberness that I have attained after seventeen years in the major leagues.

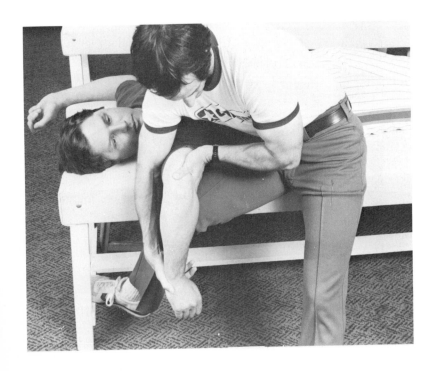

Exercise 4. To start the internal-external isometric exercises, Larry fixes my right elbow with his left hand and grabs the inside of my right wrist. He urges me to push up against his hand as far as I can without pain or discomfort and to hold that position for five or six seconds. I repeat this three to five times. Larry then switches his hand to the outside of my wrist and urges me to push against his hand in the opposite direction and to hold for five or six seconds. This, too, is repeated three to five times.

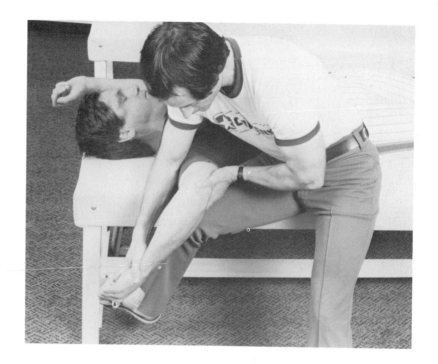

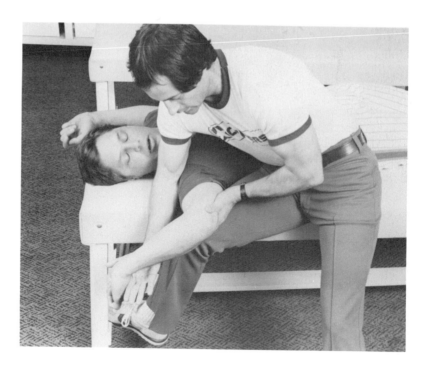

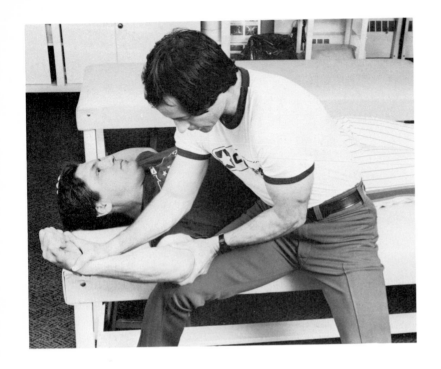

Exercise 5. To begin the second internal-external isometric rotation exercise, Larry stabilizes my elbow with his left hand and places his right hand against my wrist. I push forward in internal rotation against his resistance and try to hold this position for about five or six seconds, then relax, and repeat the exercise three to five times. The external rotation isometric is then performed, with Larry still stabilizing my elbow with his left hand but now placing his hand outside my wrist. I push back against his resistance for five or six seconds, relax, and repeat three to five times.

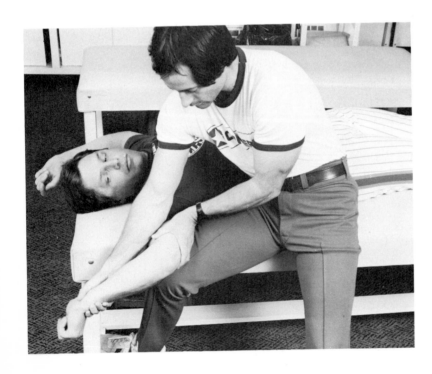

Exercise 6. The third internal-external isometric exercise begins with my elbow just off the table and my forearm perpendicular to the floor. Larry stabilizes my right elbow and forearm with his right elbow and forearm and applies pressure to the inside of my wrist. I push forward against Larry's resistance for five to six seconds, relax, and repeat three to five times. Larry then changes position and applies pressure to the outside of my right wrist with his left hand while stabilizing my shoulder and elbow with his right hand and forearm. I push back against his resistance for five to six seconds, relax, and repeat three to five times.

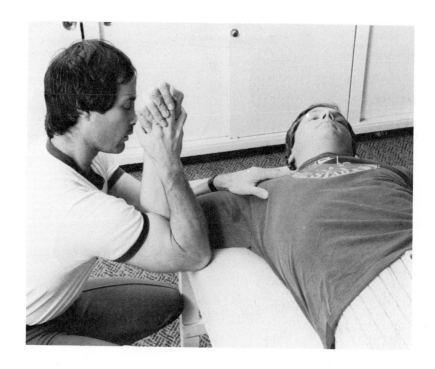

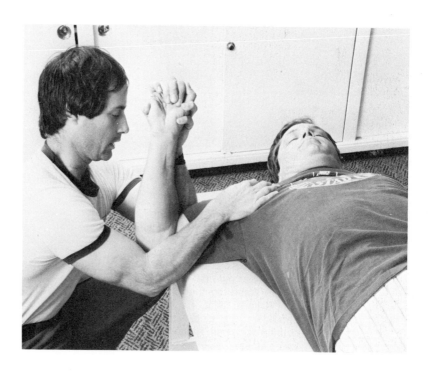

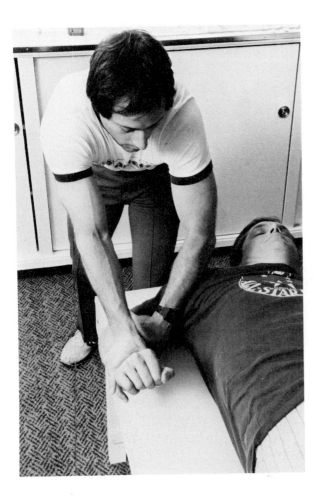

Exercise 7. For the last of the isometric exercises, my arm rests on the table in an *L*. Larry's left hand grasps my elbow while his left elbow stabilizes my shoulder. Larry applies pressure with his right hand and I push up against that resistance for a count of five. I repeat the exercise three to five times.

The four isometric exercises take about seven minutes to complete. It is then time, once again, to stretch your arm and shoulder muscles.

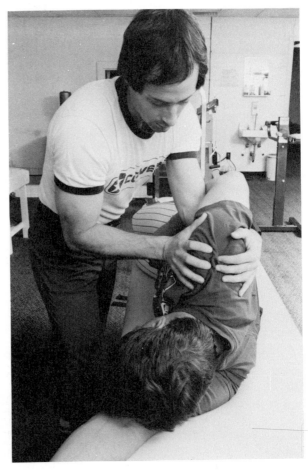

Exercise 8. To increase the circumduction of the shoulder and to get the circulation going, I start by lying on my left side. Larry's left elbow tucks under my right elbow and his fingers come together on my acromioclavicular joint. He moves the shoulder in a clockwise, then a counterclockwise, motion about five to ten times.

Exercise 9. For the overhead stretch I remain on my left side, with Larry's left hand on top of my right shoulder stabilizing the acromioclavicular joint. He applies traction to my right wrist and gradually takes my right arm back toward my forehead and pauses. By the end of the exercise, he has brought my arm back toward my head and then back to my ear.

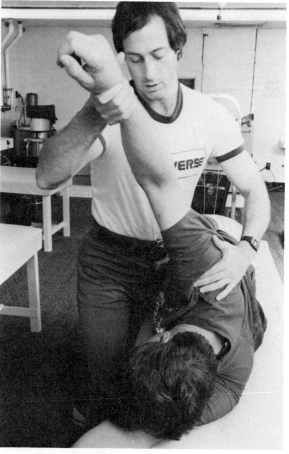

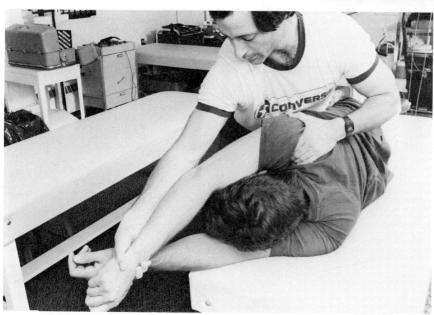

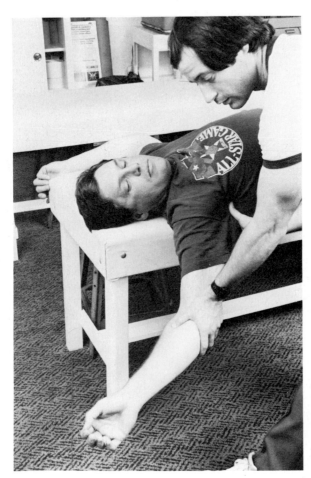

Exercise 10. Anterior shoulder stretches stretch the muscles in the front of my shoulder. Larry places his right hand under my shoulder with his fingers in my armpit to stabilize the shoulder. His left hand is at the crease of my right elbow. He moves my arm back and down toward the floor, I push back up against his resistance for four to five seconds, and then relax and return to the starting position. Repeat the exercise three or four times.

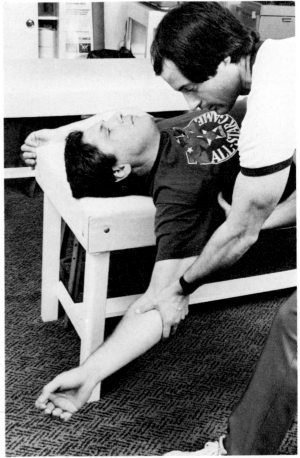

Exercise 11. The second anterior shoulder stretch begins with me on my left side. Larry places his right thumb on my acromioclavicular joint and his left wrist inside my throwing elbow. He takes my arm back in a straight line and holds the position for a few seconds. Repeat three or four times.

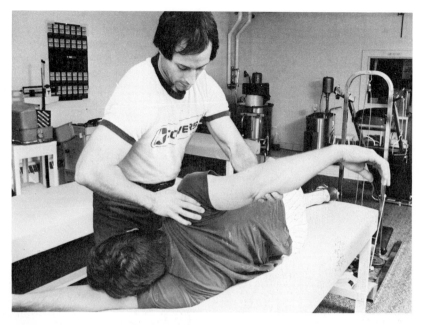

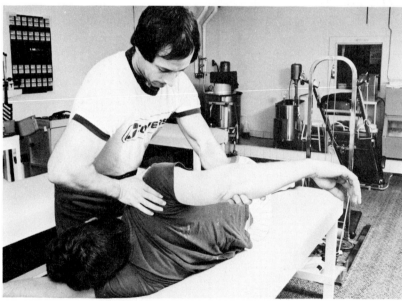

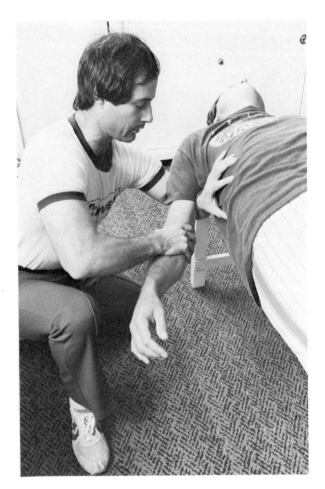

Exercise 12. The last anterior shoulder stretch begins with me lying on my back and my right arm and shoulder just barely off the table's edge. Larry slides his left arm under my right arm and through the armpit and places his left hand against my chest. Using his arm as a fulcrum, Larry takes my arm back perpendicular to my body and holds it in full extension for three or four seconds. The exercise is repeated three to five times.

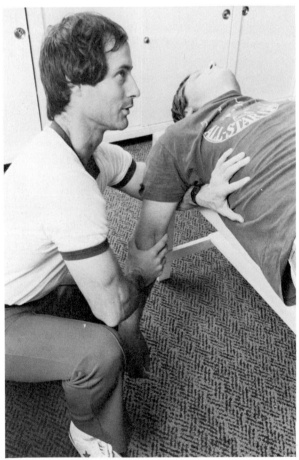

Exercise 13. I perform two internal rotator stretches lying facedown on the trainer's table. In the first, Larry stabilizes my scapula and elbow with his right hand and forearm. For a count of five to ten seconds, Larry brings my right arm up toward my head. In the second stretch, Larry frees my scapula and brings my arm up toward his body as he holds me in position for five to ten seconds. Repeat three to five times.

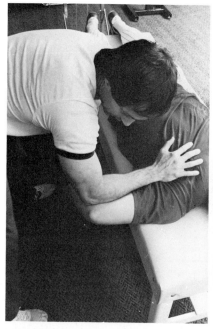

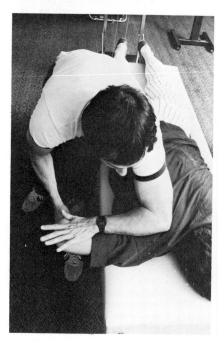

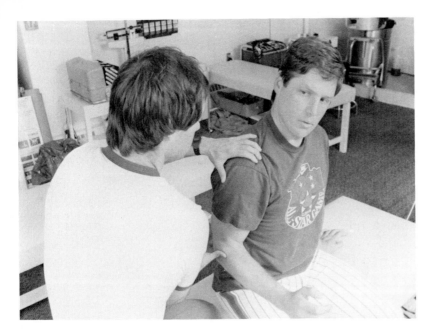

Exercise 14. I begin the upper-arm stretch sitting on the table. Larry places his left hand on my acromioclavicular joint, applying firm pressure with his left thumb over the contour of the back of the shoulder. His right hand grasps my upper arm just above the bend of my elbow and I raise my upper arm in a backward motion against Larry's pressure. Repeat three to five times.

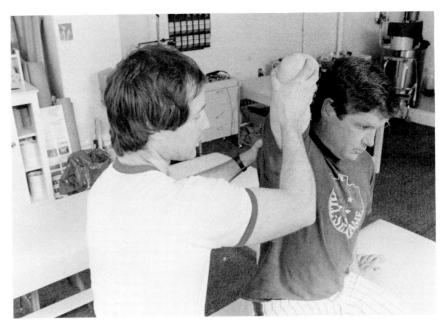

Exercise 15. For an anterior stretch prior to the supraspinatus isometric exercise, Larry brings my arms backward as far as they can go and tries to have me touch my hands behind my back. During a warm-up, I bring the arms forward to clap hands as Larry applies resistance to the inside part of my elbows. Repeat three to five times.

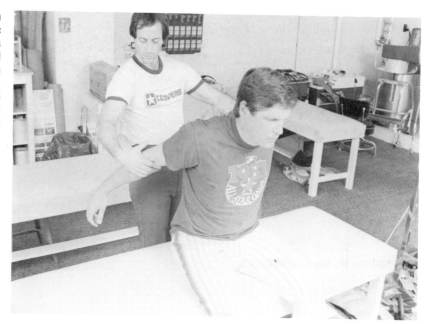

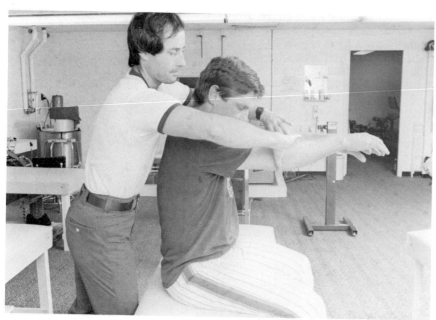

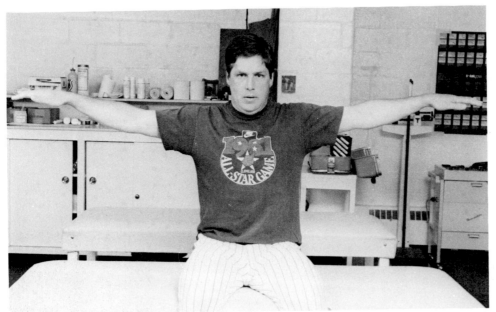

Exercise 16. In the isometric exercise for the supraspinatus muscle, I hold my arms outstretched while sitting on the table. I rotate my arms internally so my thumbs face downward, and I bring my arms forward about thirty degrees. Larry applies resistance to both elbows as I push down. Try to avoid shrugging your shoulders so you are certain to be strengthening the key supraspinatus muscle at the top of your rotator cuff. Hold for about five to six seconds and then repeat the exercise three to five times.

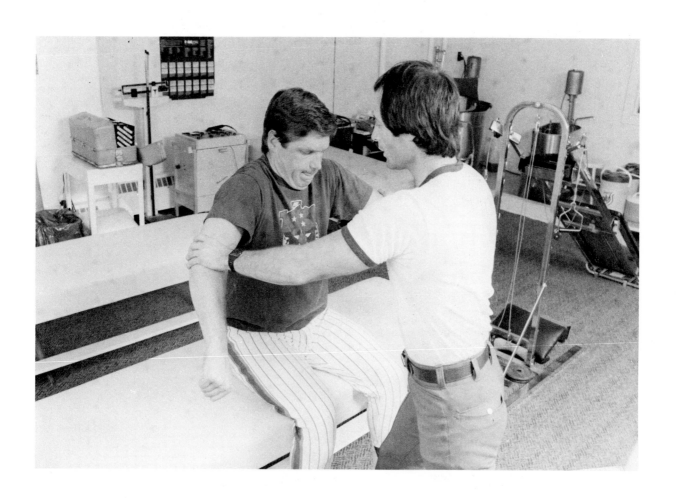

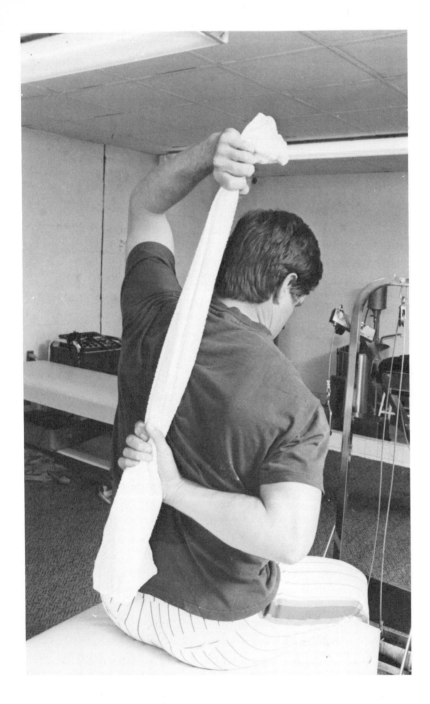

Exercise 17. This exercise will increase flexibility in both the pitching and off-side arms. The right upper arm and shoulder in a right-handed pitcher are understandably more flexible than the left upper arm and shoulder. To further enhance your flexibility on the right side, grasp a towel behind your back with your right hand. Pull up with your left arm and hand. If you want to increase your left side flexibility, simply reverse the towel and pull up with your right arm and hand.

arm and shoulder. You want to build up a sweat so the muscles are warm and ready to be stretched.

Warm-up of the external rotators in Exercise 1 is very important for me and probably for most starting pitchers. Our internal rotator muscles are very strong from repeating the forward motion of pitching. The antagonistic external rotators are weaker and I therefore work these muscles more in these exercises. I am not saying that all starters will find this true, but I know from experience what my needs are. Every day, rain or shine, during the season, I have these rotators warmed up, lightly stretched, exercised with isometric pressure, and stretched again at the end. The only break from this norm is that once the season is well under way and I notice a degree of fatigue in my throwing arm, I will periodically take a day off and give my rotator cuff a day of rest.

Larry Mayol has a nice analogy that compares the internal rotators to an automobile's accelerator and the external rotators to its brakes. "If you drive a six-hundred-horsepower car without any brakes," Larry suggests, "sooner or later, you are going to have car trouble if you can only bring the engine forward and not bring it to a stop."

Once I have been warmed up and lightly stretched, Larry runs me through some basic isometric exercises (numbers 4, 5, 6, and 7) that cover the whole range of the pitching motion. We do each of these isometric exercises two or three times, holding the extended position to the count of five.

These isometric exercises take no more than seven minutes, but they do wonders for the strengthening of the pitching apparatus. The manual assistance assures that the key elbow joint is stabilized and that the shoulder muscles are isolated so that genuine strengthening of the rotator-cuff muscles occurs.

Exercise 8, which increases the circumduction (moving around) of the shoulder, can only be done with professional assistance.

Exercise 9, and virtually all the remaining stretches, I do through a complete range of motion. I repeat most of these exercises five to ten times, but the beginner should not be that ambitious.

Also with Larry's assistance, I do stretches that keep the pectoral muscles in my chest strong and flexible. In the anterior shoulder stretch, the front part of my shoulder and the point where the rotator inserts into my humerus are stretched. Larry again keeps my elbow stabilized to avoid slippage. Because of the strength I have developed from constant throwing, I can move my arm almost 360 degrees through this exercise.

To repeat my constant warning against imitation, youngsters should not strive to duplicate my movement and feel discouraged if they cannot match it. Every physique is different and your body structure and throwing motion will greatly influence the range of movement with which you start these exercises. If you lack the initial flexibility and strength to do this work, a good trainer or knowledgeable physical therapist can use a "contract-relax" method that enables you to increase your range of motion with his assistance. As time goes on and you faithfully work on these drills, you will likely find that you can achieve the desired ends by your own efforts.

Each pitcher will have his own endurance level for these exercises. Accept a low starting point, if necessary, and work honestly to achieve a higher level of strength and flexibility. As in the weight work, cheating your way through by momentum will fool no one but yourself.

Larry often assists me with Exercise 16, which isolates the supraspinatus muscle, the vital rotator-cuff muscle that holds the shoulder in a fixed position to the humerus. If you are experiencing discomfort in this area, you will have the sickening feeling of being unable to keep your arms outstretched at all.

The final exercise I do on the trainer's table stretches and exercises my left arm and shoulder, which normally for a right-handed pitcher are much less flexible than his throwing arm and shoulder. Exercise 17 can be performed all year round to increase suppleness in your off side.

This is a program that has worked for me, but I do not offer it as a total guarantee of improved performance or as an absolute guide to follow slavishly. I do maintain, however, that building equal strength through the whole range of motion in your rotator cuff and adjacent shoulder muscles will cut down the chance of injury and enable you to focus more on the mental and spiritual aspects of pitching. The entire process—warm-ups, manually assisted exercises, and stretches—doesn't take more than a half-hour, but I assure you that it is time as well spent as any activity in the life of a pitcher.

Throwing Between Starts

Throughout most of my career, I never threw on the day after I pitched. I ran my twenty wind sprints in the outfield and played pepper to keep my reflexes sharp.

Under the tutelage of pitching savant George Bamberger, who was my Mets manager and pitching coach at the start of the 1983 season, I changed my routine last year. George believes that a pitcher should throw every day, even if he has started the day before. If you run every day to keep the legs in shape, George argues, you should throw every day to keep the arm in shape.

I incorporated George's advice in 1983. I now throw the day after I start. It's just catch in the outfield, lobbing the ball between fifty and seventy feet for about ten to twelve minutes, but it definitely helps me. Here is another example of the importance of being flexible and open to new ideas. Throwing in the outfield nicely supplements my work with manually assisted exercises. The combination works well to alleviate the stiffness in my back, arm, and lower body that is natural after a pitching effort.

On the second day after a start, it is traditional for a starting pitcher to throw more seriously. In the old days, I threw in the outfield with my pitching coach. He stood on the right-field foul line and I lobbed the ball to him from about fifty feet away toward right center. I then backed up farther into the outfield until I reached a point where I felt I would have to overthrow to reach him. Twelve to twenty minutes of throwing sufficed on this day. The variation in time depended on whether I had thrown a high number of pitches in my last start and was stiffer than usual, or if my next start was scheduled on the fourth, fifth, or sixth day.

Under the new regimen I started in 1983, I still throw for up to twenty minutes but divide the time between eight to ten minutes of catch in the outfield and eight to ten minutes on the pitching mound in the bullpen. After years of experience, I know how much throwing I need to do and when I should stop. To reiterate, I do not suggest that you follow my program exactly. Every pitcher must find out what kind of preparation between starts works best for him.

Under the new program, I follow the same routine on the third day after a starting assignment that I follow on day 2. I do my fifteen to twenty wind sprints, play pepper, and do twenty minutes of throwing, divided between catch in the outfield and work on the bullpen mound. As the season goes along, I may cut down on the mound work because I do not feel the work will improve my pitching skills. The important aspect becomes getting physically ready for the next start. By doing the isometrics regularly, I feel my strength can be maintained without a great deal of throwing from the bullpen mound.

On the day before a start, I do no throwing off the bullpen mound. I play a game of light catch in the outfield, just as I used to do in the front yard as a kid. Baseball is a serious business in the professional ranks, but it is also a game. A pitcher should never lose sight of that. He should prepare himself mentally by relaxing and just playing a little game of catch.

Now that you know something of the physical world of the pitcher, let's apply that knowledge to a major-league game. Baseball theory always makes more sense when applied to a specific context.

9 THE ART OF PITCHING

Baseball is fascinating because it can be probed on so many levels: the career of a great player, the season of a great team, a magnificent play-off or World Series, a key series during a pennant race, or even just one game. It doesn't have to be a meaningful game in the standings. Drama is inherent in any game of baseball because of its marvelous symmetry, much of it connected to the integer three.

Every game is divided into early, middle, and late innings. Every batting order is divided into top, middle, and bottom thirds (which is why the modern innovation of the designated hitter is so destructive to baseball's natural rhythms). And every half-inning has three outs that the pitcher must register if he is to succeed.

Now, why don't you join me on the mound for a game during the 1983 championship season of the National League. The Mets were mired in the cellar of the National League Eastern Division, but our opponents were the defending World Champion St. Louis Cardinals. Every team gets up to play the champs, and this particular series had special interest because it was the first meeting of the teams since a blockbuster deal had been completed one week earlier on the eve of the June 15 trading deadline.

The Mets had acquired Keith Hernandez, an All-Star first baseman, in exchange for the talented pitcher Neil Allen. The night before my start, Neil had thrown eight innings of shutout ball against his former teammates on the way to a 6–0 victory. The Cardinals now had a 2–1 edge in this unusual six-game series that had been necessitated by a rash of rainouts earlier in the season.

As I mentally readied myself for my start, my goals were to even the series at two apiece and to attempt to pitch a complete game to provide our bullpen with at least one game of rest. I would be pitching the first game of a twi-night doubleheader, the second in three days for our staff. We would be facing three more twin bills in the next two weeks before the All-Star Game holiday, so I vowed to make every effort to pitch a complete game.

The starting time for the first game was 5:35 P.M., so I arrived at the ballpark at 2:30, about a half-hour after I normally would on a day when I wasn't pitching. I changed into my uniform and had Larry Mayol do a few stretches with me, but not as many or as strenuous as ones he would do on a day between starts.

I returned to my locker and mulled over the data I had been collecting on the Cardinals over the past week. I had read every Cardinal box score in the newspapers since the big trade. I noticed that the team was not hitting very well. The weekend before they arrived at Shea, the Cards had lost two out of three at home to the surging Chicago Cubs. After beating the curve-balling right-hander Chuck Rainey on Friday, 5–4, driving Chuck out with a barrage of doubles in the fourth inning, the Cards had been shut down, 10–1 and 4–1, the next two weekend afternoons.

Cub southpaw Steve Trout, who has a good running fastball and fine control of his breaking pitches, had four-hit the Cards in the 10–1 game. He had a shutout going into the ninth inning when a new member of the Cardinals, Floyd Rayford, pinch-hit a home run. I didn't know Rayford, but we have an active grapevine in major-league baseball. Advance scouts follow a team at least one series before it is scheduled to face us. Advance-scouting information is particularly useful for hitters that you have never seen before. Dave Madison, the Met scout who had been following the Cards, indicated to me that Rayford was a good fastball hitter who had trouble with breaking pitches away. Some teammates who had played with Rayford in the International League or had heard the American League

This is a copy of the chart kept by pitcher Ed Lynch in the Mets' dug-out: Tom Seaver working against the St. Louis Cardinals at Shea Stadium, June 22, 1983.

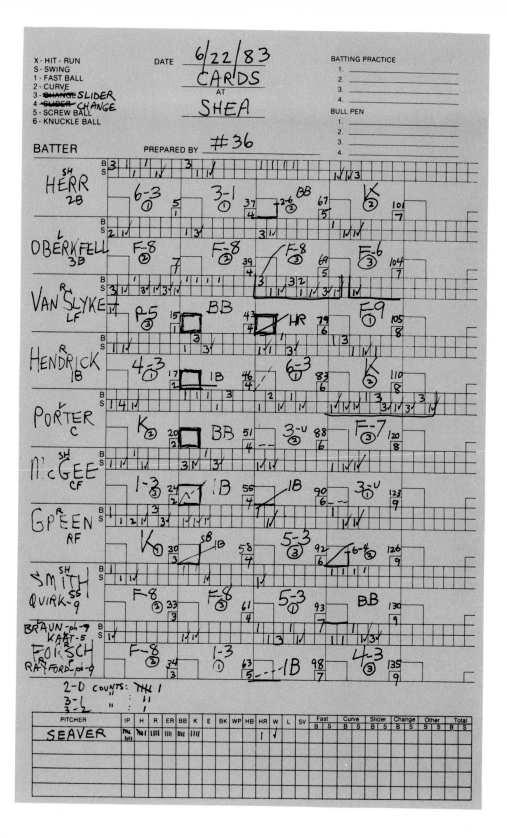

grapevine about him confirmed Dave's analysis. Dave also provided me with an important piece of news. Dane Iorg, the Cardinals' excellent utility outfielder and a fine fastball-hitting pinch hitter, had a sprained wrist and would not be playing against us in New York.

I also asked around if anybody had seen the Cardinals' rookie phenom, Andy Van Slyke, play. Van Slyke had been burning up the American Association for the Cardinals' farm team in Louisville, and had been installed in Keith Hernandez's number-three slot in the batting order immediately after the trade. I noticed in the box scores that Van Slyke had hit an occasional double, but had yet to slug one over the fence in the big leagues. The Mets don't have an American Association farm team so no one had recent information, but Keith Hernandez had played with Van Slyke in spring training. "He likes the ball down and in," Keith advised, "but you may give him trouble on the outside part of the plate."

In addition to my scouts' and my teammates' insights and my own reading of box scores, I had another mental advantage in preparing for my start. I had been able to observe the Cardinals take batting practice the previous two evenings as well as watch them play three games. Baseball is often a game of little edges, and indications; tendencies in a hitter's stroke that you pick up in batting practice can tell you what kind of groove he is in. I remember when Billy Williams was playing with the Cubs. If he was swinging for the fences in batting practice, his timing was usually off in the game. But if he was using that sweet swing of his to drive "frozen ropes" for base hits all over the field, I was certain that I would have my hands full in the game.

Baseball fans can get clues to the course of a game by coming out early to watch batting practice. They say that the night he hit three homers in the final World Series game of 1977, Reggie Jackson blasted balls all over the park in pregame bp including one that bounced off the top of the right-field bleachers and out of Yankee Stadium.

During this series so far, I had noticed that George Hendrick, though leading the league in batting average and always a power threat, was lunging at low pitches out of the strike zone that he normally would take. Willie McGee, another Cardinal outfielder, not as powerful as Hendrick but a very swift runner who knew how to use his speed, didn't seem comfortable at the plate. He did not seem to be hitting inside pitches with any authority, either in bp or in the game. I saw Andy Van Slyke crush a few batting-practice pitches over the fence, and saw the accuracy of Keith Hernandez's analysis of the rookie. You came down and in to Van Slyke at your own risk, but it looked as though he could be handled on the outside corner.

The Cardinals had won the first game of the series, 3–1, despite a strong performance by our right-handed starter, Craig Swan. The Cardinals seemed to be in a team slump. They had been two-hit the day before in St. Louis by the curveballing Cub right-hander Dick Ruthven. On the other hand, as befits defending world champions, they showed an ability to strike quickly when an opportunity arose.

Craig had only one bad inning against the Cards, the fourth, when they scored all three runs, but it cost him the game. I had watched as Craig made too good a pitch on the outside corner to George Hendrick on an 0–2 count. George stuck his bat out and got a game-tying double. I reminded myself that when my turn came, I must get George to chase a bad pitch, especially if I got ahead in the count.

I then had seen Darrell Porter, the Cardinals' left-handed hitting catcher and a strong pull hitter, drive a pitch in his wheelhouse to right for the go-ahead run. I remembered that Porter can be fooled on change-of-speed pitches, and I made a mental note to myself that I would not try to throw the hummer past Darrell before setting him up with off-speed pitches.

With Porter on second and two out, and still only one run behind, I wondered about giving David Green, another hard-hitting Cardinal outfielder, anything good to hit with the weak-hitting shortstop, Ozzie Smith, on deck. Swannie decided to go after Green, and made a pitch too good. Green singled up the middle for the third run of the inning and a run that turned out to be a big insurance tally in the game.

Green is a budding star, the player that Whitey Herzog insisted on obtaining before he made the big deal in which the Milwaukee Brewers received Ted Simmons, Pete Vuckovich, and Rollie Fingers. As the series unfolded, it became apparent that Green would be the hottest Cardinal, a piece of information that Swannie, opening the series, did not have the luxury of knowing. Green went on to hit his first home run of the 1983 season in the second game of the doubleheader, although the Mets came from behind to win, 6–4. I had seen Green collect two more hits in the next game, and I decided that I would have to pitch Green carefully. I wouldn't be afraid to throw him fastballs, but I would establish early in each at-bat the inside part of the plate. At all costs, I didn't want David digging in on me at the plate and being able to drive the ball all over the field.

It was now a few minutes after 5:00 P.M. on a warm Wednesday afternoon in New York, the first full day of summer. Accompanied by my bullpen coach, Gene Dusan, I left the clubhouse and walked down the underground tunnel toward our bullpen behind the right-field fence. I walked out to the bullpen and started throwing a few easy tosses to Gene about fifty feet away. He backed up to about seventy feet to receive a few more tosses from me, and then I stepped on the mound and prepared my twenty minutes of warm-up throwing. It was a sunshiny day, warm but not oppressive with humidity. I looked up to see the stadium lights already turned on, but they wouldn't have much effect until late in my game. Perhaps I would have an advantage throwing into the advancing shadows of dusk. I knew from experience that a glare off the center-field background for the hitters might aid me. Some batters could have trouble picking up the changes of speed in my pitches while others might find it hard to follow the rotation on the ball.

I knew that my mental preparation for the Cardinals had been adequate. I reminded myself that I must pitch within myself. I no longer was the kind of pitcher who could accelerate his fastball, make it "rise" time and again to bail himself out of tough situations. I had to use more guile than earlier in my career and capitalize on the understanding that comes with experience of what is working best on a given day.

I felt that my stuff was moving adequately in the bullpen, but as I said long ago in these pages, I never trust the bullpen experience for anything but loosening up my muscles. I was ready. It was proving time.

I trotted out to the mound as the crowd slowly gathered at Shea. This was a makeup doubleheader, not on the original schedule. While nearly twenty thousand fans would come to the park that night, we didn't have half that many at the start. The crowd in New York is always enthusiastic no matter what its size, and I was happy to be pitching in front of it again. But I have learned to rein my emotional response to the fans. I don't work well when my emotions are too up-front. I started to concentrate on my job: pitching—I hoped—nine victorious innings, for the New York Mets against the St. Louis Cardinals.

Once the national anthem had been played, I walked around the mound, housekeeping, making sure that there were no imperfections in the dirt. I briskly threw my eight warm-up pitches. I was ready. Come with me now to the mound to follow the action pitch-by-pitch.

Tommy Herr, the Cardinals' peppery switch-hitting second baseman, leads off. He's a dead fastball hitter, so I decide to show him a slider as my first pitch. It moves inside for ball one. I then crank out my first fastball, but it tails outside for ball two. Wonderful! Two pitches and I'm already behind 2–0. What was that about "always get ahead in the count"? Sometimes practice is a lot harder than preaching!

All right, I'm in a 2–0 hole, but I guess that Tommy will take the next pitch because a leadoff hitter always wants to get on base and he's only two pitches from a free ticket. I'm right, Tommy's taking, and this time, my four-seam fastball tails in on the outside corner for a 2–1 count. But I miss on a sinker, so I'm in a 3–1 hole with the very first batter.

I now calculate that Tommy will be swinging, trying to pull the ball into right field, either down the line sharply or into the gap in right center. I am determined that he won't get a pitch to pull. I muscle up like the old days and throw him a rising fastball. It's a good pitch, it moves well, and Tommy grounds out routinely to our shortstop, Jose Oquendo, for a 6–3 putout. One down.

Ken Oberkfell, Cardinal third baseman and another left-handed hitter, steps in. Ken is not the kind of big power hitter that third basemen usually are, but he does like the ball inside. I decide to go outside to his weakness with my first pitch, a curveball. It crosses the outside corner for strike one. I notice that plate umpire Charlie Williams is giving me a good part of the outside corner. That means I'll have a wide strike zone today unless Charlie changes in midstream. He doesn't; good umpires consistently maintain their idea of the strike zone.

Ahead 0–1 on Ken, I try a tailing fastball. He's behind the ball and lifts a routine fly to center where Mookie Wilson gathers it in. Two up, two down, on seven pitches. Hey, this is easy!

Up steps rookie Andy Van Slyke for our first confrontation.

Andy is coming off a game last night where he had blasted his first major-league home run. I know that he wants another now to get his team off quickly. I figure that he's expecting a fastball, so I start him off with a slider at the place where he's least expecting it, at his strength, down and in. He takes it for strike one. I then move outside with a tailing fastball that he fouls off to make the count 0–2. I try a sinker, but it falls too low. At 1–2, our battle really begins.

He keeps fouling off the four-seam outside fastballs and inside sliders that I alternately throw him. I am careful not to test his inside strength with a hummer in a scoreless ball game. I finally win the lengthy battle by getting him to pop to third on a rising fastball off the outside corner. Three up, three down, on fifteen pitches. I'll take that any time!

When I return to the mound to start the second inning, I'm three runs to the good, thanks to a three-run homer belted by our outstanding rookie outfielder, Darryl Strawberry, off Cardinal starter Bob Forsch. Although I always give my best effort regardless of the score, it is nice to have some runs. I haven't had many to work with so far in 1983, and you have more margin for error when you realize that you don't have to pitch a shutout to have a chance to win.

I also remind myself, however, not to relax with a lead. As I lightly toss my warm-up pitches before the start of the inning, I flash back to the time early in my career when I lost a big lead in a game against Juan Marichal and the San Francisco Giants. I remember how Gil Hodges called me into the manager's office the next day and pointed out my mistake. "You must always stay in the game mentally," Gil chastised me. "Your concentration must never lapse, because you can't turn it on and off like a faucet." I had let the Giants back into that game, and when they brought the tying run to the plate, I was emotionally unable to stem their rally. I vowed that tonight I would not make the same mistake.

Returning to the challenge of the moment, I prepare to face the Cardinals' cleanup hitter George Hendrick, who has become their regular first baseman since the Hernandez trade. I've already talked about what a good hitter George is. He may not talk to the press, but he sure talks to us pitchers with his bat, and the message usually is not kind. George is worthy of comparison to the late, great Roberto Clemente. Like Clemente,

George can cover virtually the entire strike zone with his quick bat. Also like Clemente, George will often give a pitcher the lower four-inch square of the outside corner, his way of communicating his doubt that a pitcher can be so fine that he can consistently hit that lowest target in the strike zone.

As I mentioned earlier, I had observed so far in this series that George had been chasing a lot of low-breaking pitches out of the strike zone. I keep this note in the back of my mind, but I start George off with a fastball down the middle for strike one. He then chases my outside sinker and hits it off the end of the bat to our second baseman, Brian Giles. It's an easy out, 4–3, one down.

Up steps left-hand-hitting Darrell Porter, the Cardinal catcher and the MVP in both the 1982 World Series and the National League Championship Series. This season Darrell has been showing signs of making the adjustment to National League pitching after years of success with Kansas City. He has an open stance and likes the ball inside, so I decide to go to his weakness and throw a sailing fastball. He takes it for strike one. I then fool him with my first change-up of the game, which he takes for strike two.

I now feel that I have Darrell at my mercy on the 0–2 count. I decide that he is least expecting a pitch to his strength, the inside fastball. I throw it and it moves well, into Darrell, and he swings and misses for my first strikeout of the game. Striking out a good hitter on three pitches is not very common, but I was able to get Darrell this time because of the change-up on pitch two. It left him off-stride for the fastball that immediately followed.

Switch-hitting center fielder Willie McGee steps up. Despite his batting slump, McGee remains dangerous. He's slightly built, but he has deceptive strength if you give him a pitch in his wheelhouse. He hit two home runs in Game 3 of the 1982 World Series. His hands are very quick with the bat even if, so far, they have been slow during this series. He also gets a lot of leg hits by hitting down on the ball and using his superior speed.

My fastball is moving well tonight, so I start Willie off with an inside hummer that he swings at and misses for strike one. I decelerate my fastball slightly and throw it toward the outside corner. Willie fouls it back, so again I'm ahead 0–2. With Willie in a slump and my fastball working well, I decide to stick with the number one to get either a strikeout or a groundout. I throw him a hard sinker, faster than the 0–1 pitch, and he grounds routinely to second base for the third out. Six up, six down, on only twenty-four pitches. If you can keep yourself from averaging more than fifteen pitches an inning, you usually have a good shot at a complete game. So far, so good, for me tonight.

Still leading 3–0, I face the hot David Green to begin the third inning. I decide to keep him honest at the plate and go right after his "kitchen" with a hummer. But it moves too far inside, for ball one. I come right back with an outside fastball that he takes for strike one. I get ahead of him with an outside curve that he lets go for strike two.

I then shift my attack to sliders since I expect that he is guessing that I'm coming back in with my fastball. I throw him a down and away slider that he takes for ball two, and then repeat the same pitch, again surmising that he is guessing fastball. My strategy works, because David is called out on strikes for the seventh straight out that I have registered. Some part of me must be saying, "It can't be this easy!" but on the surface, everything is smooth. I'm just doing what I know I can do.

Ozzie Smith steps up to the plate. The brilliant-fielding shortstop has looked fatigued to me throughout this series. He hasn't been quick with his bat head in the prior games or in batting practice. I vow that Ozzie will get only fastballs until he proves that he can hit one with authority. On a 1–1 count, he flies out routinely to center field for out number two.

The good-hitting pitcher Bob Forsch steps up. He's one of the many major leaguers from that baseball hotbed of Sacramento, California (his brother Ken, Larry Bowa, Steve Sax, and Dick Ruthven are just a few of the others). Forsch had delivered a sacrifice fly in his last start, a winning effort against the Cubs, and in his career, he has hit several home runs. I decide that he still won't be able to connect with my riser tonight. I jam him and Bob also flies out to center. I throw only ten pitches in the third inning, just thirty-four for the game so far.

When I head out for the fourth inning, I have a 6–0 lead as my mates have knocked Bob Forsch out in the bottom of the third. The second time around a batting order is always a crucial phase of a game as the batters show how or if they have adjusted to the pitcher's strength this given game. I start off leadoff man Tommy Herr with another slider that he takes for a ball. But I go after with him with fastballs, and on the second one, he grounds to Keith Hernandez wide of first. Knowing Herr's a fast man, I quickly get over near the bag, take Keith's toss, tag first with my right foot, and register the first out of the fourth.

I start off Kenny Oberkfell with a sinking inside fastball that he takes for strike one. Having curved him during his first at-bat, I decide to surprise him with a slider. It breaks sharply in, as I want, and he hits the ball on the handle of the bat, a routine fly to center field. Two up, two down, eleven straight outs in the game, but I'm not concentrating on perfect streaks, but on how to deal with Andy Van Slyke for the second time. As I said, every baseball game has a beginning, a middle, and an end. Little did I know as I rubbed up the ball to face Andy that I was heading momentarily into my first stormy section of the game.

I have nobody to blame but myself. I throw four straight fastballs out of the strike zone to Van Slyke. It doesn't matter whether I throw a sinker or a riser; every one of them misses badly. My catcher, Junior Ortiz, gestures to me with his hands down as if to say, "Keep the ball down." I now face George Hendrick and make a mental mistake.

I throw George three outside pitches in a row. He takes the first one, a fastball, for strike one, and then watches a slider go outside for ball one. I come back with another outside slider, not a bad pitch, but I had not established the inside corner during this at-bat. (I see this now, of course, in hindsight, which is 20–20, as we all know.) George is dug in at the plate and he strokes my second straight slider solidly to right field for a single.

Darrell Porter moves in to the batter's box, and for the second time in the inning, I lose my perception of the strike zone with a left-hander batting. I fall behind on three straight fastballs. With Darrell taking on 3–0, I manage to get a hummer over the plate for strike one. But not willing to throw another fast one that he might be "sitting" on, I try a slider that misses low and in for ball four. The bases are loaded, thanks to my unforgivable gifts of two free passes.

I quickly get ahead of Willie McGee with a down and in slider that he takes for strike one. I then throw the tailing fastball that has good movement away and Willie fouls it back. I'm back in the driver's seat with an 0–2 count. I try to get Willie to chase a fastball even farther outside than the previous pitch, but he takes it for ball one.

Thinking that Willie is expecting me to stay outside, I decide to go for either the strikeout or a weak grounder with an inside slider. It's a good pitch, it "bites" nicely, but Willie's bat is coming alive. He gets around on it and beats it into the ground. It bounces over my head and in front of second base. With Willie's speed, no one can make a play. One run scores and the bases remain loaded. The Cardinals, still five runs down, are not taking baserunning chances.

David Green digs in. I fanned him last inning, but that seems like a very long time ago. I quickly get ahead of him on two fastballs that he first misses and then fouls off. "I still have my good stuff," I tell myself. "I've gotten ahead of two good hitters, 0–2. Now finish him off this time!"

Confident that David cannot handle my fastball, I try to ride the ball up and in, but I get it out over the plate too much. David drills it into right-center for a two-run single to cut the lead to 6–3. The tying run is coming to the plate, and I cannot blame my manager, Frank Howard, for heating up the bullpen.

My lead has been cut in half in a few pitches, but all is not lost. I have been getting ahead of the last two hitters, and my ball is moving well. I remind myself that the due batter, Ozzie Smith, will still get nothing but fastballs from me. I fall behind 2–0, and David Green steals second on the second pitch to give the Cardinals two runners in scoring position. A bad pitch to Ozzie now would make the score 6–5. But I suppress any negative thoughts, and fire a third fastball to Ozzie. He hits a soft fly to center that Mookie Wilson gathers in for the third out. I throw twenty-four pitches in the fourth inning and lose half of my lead. But on the bright side, I am still ahead, 6–3.

As I go downstairs to the clubhouse to change my shirts between innings, I think to myself, Oh, those bases on balls! Many a manager has muttered these words on his deathbed, and for good reason. My comfortable lead had begun to evaporate because I walked Andy Van Slyke with two out and no one on base. Van Slyke would have had to hit a six-run homer to tie the game, and I pitched around him! Then I compounded the felony by walking Darrell Porter to load the bases. In the big leagues, perhaps as many as 75 percent of the walks become runs. It is no surprise that in major-league clubhouses, you will hear pitchers grouse, "It seems every time we walk someone, they score."

It is such a basic truth to avoid walking people. You always have to throw more pitches when you walk batters. Even if they don't score, you are making pitches that you could save for key situations late in the ball game.

Well, nobody's perfect, I console myself as I return to the dugout. As I start out for the fifth inning, I think positively. By retiring Ozzie Smith to end the fourth, I have assured that the pitcher will lead off for the Cardinals. He is now Jim Kaat, the amazing forty-four-year-old relief pitcher, who is a good hitter for a pitcher. But I handle him on fastballs. He tries a drag bunt on an 0–1 pitch, but he pushes it right at me. I pick it up and throw to first for an easy 1–3 putout.

Tommy Herr comes up for the third time and I decide to go after him with fastballs right away. The strategy doesn't work because for the third time in less than two innings, I lose sight of the strike zone for a left-handed hitter. Maybe I am not picking up the target correctly for lefties. Whatever the reason, I walk Tommy on four straight errant fastballs.

Keith Hernandez walks to the mound and gives me a tip. "Whitey [Herzog, Cardinals' manager] will try to run his way back into the ball game," Keith advises. "Be alive!" My battery mate, Junior Ortiz, is on his toes for a potential steal of second by Tommy Herr. With left-handed hitter Ken Oberkfell at the plate, Junior's view of second base is slightly blocked. Despite being down three runs in the score, the Cardinals might very well steal in this situation.

I throw a slider that breaks away from Ken. Sure enough, Herr is running, and for some reason—perhaps he has missed a sign—Oberkfell takes the pitch for a ball. Junior comes up firing and throws a strike to Jose Oquendo, low and on the bag. Herr is out and there are two down, none on.

Buoyed by the fine defensive play, I go after Kenny with the same tailing fastball that had retired him twice previously. For the third time in a row, he makes mediocre contact and lifts an easy fly to center. Mookie grabs it for the third out. Not a 1–2–3 inning, but thanks to Junior's bullet to second base, it is the equivalent of three up and three down. I throw only eight pitches in the fifth. Dusk is deepening and the batters may be seeing the ball a little better with the lights taking effect. But I feel strong and encouraged by the easy inning.

The Cardinals are stifling our offense, so it is still 6–3 as I start the sixth and face Andy Van Slyke for a third time. I had thrown him all fastballs the last time, when he started all the trouble with a walk. I decide to start him off with a slider that breaks low and in for ball one. I return to my fastball strength and get ahead of him 1–2 as he fouls off a riser on the fists for strike one and is fooled by a sinker that he takes on the outside corner for strike two.

A humdinger of a battle now commences. Ahead in the count, I decide to surprise Andy with a curve, which he hasn't seen all day, but it breaks high and outside to make it 2–2. I try the sinker again, but he gets a piece of it to stay alive. He doesn't bite at another curve that stays outside, which brings the count to 3–2. I try an outside rising fastball, but he chops it foul to hang in there.

"Give the rookie credit for making you work," I tell myself as I turn my back to Andy and rub up the new baseball that Junior has given me from Charlie Williams. "I know his strength is low and inside, but maybe he'll be guessing outside now, after all the pitches I've just thrown in that location," I reason. I shake off Junior's fastball sign and get the slider signal. I wind up and deliver. I get the slider where I want to—down and in—but it's a flat pitch. It doesn't have the good sharp movement in the hitting zone. *Thwack!* I hear Andy connect solidly with the ball, and in the twinkling of an eye, the ball is bouncing in the Met bullpen. Andy has clubbed his second home run in two games, and my lead is down to two runs.

As I rub up the new baseball Junior Ortiz has thrown me, I have to ask myself some hard questions. "Am I getting tired? Did I drop my elbow before I threw the slider? Why did I let this happen?" I have failed to get the important first out of the inning and have lost a run of my lead.

I then gather myself together and start to think positively about the next hitter, George Hendrick. I remember my mistake in the last at-bat and begin establishing the inside corner on George with my first pitch, a good running fastball that tails into him for a foul strike one. After two more fastballs into his "kitchen," I have George lunging on a slider that he hits routinely to short for the first out of inning number six.

I quickly get ahead of Darrell Porter this time with a tailing fastball for called strike one. He takes a curve to even the count at 1–1, but the off-speed pitch has served its purpose. Darrell is off-balance for the rest of the at-bat, and on a 2–2 count, he hits a sinker to Keith Hernandez for an easy unassisted putout.

Willie McGee steps in. He had gotten the Cards' first RBI in his last at-bat, and he may be breaking out of his slump. You never know when a professional hitter is ready to turn it around. Willie is obviously getting his act together, because on an 0–1 pitch, he rips a good sinker up the middle for his second straight single. For the first time since I got the lead, I now face the potential tying run in the person of David Green, a very hot hitter. His strength is the fastball, but so is mine. I'm not going to give in to him by offering less than my best, but I plan to move the ball around him and vary my speeds. He takes a riser high and away for ball one, but he grounds the next pitch, a sinker, easily to Hubie Brooks at third, who throws to first for the inning-ending out. I feel satisfied that I have not let Van Slyke's home run ruffle me. I have thrown ninety-two pitches in six innings, but still feel strong.

The Mets do not answer the home run, so it is 6–4 as I start the top of the seventh. Ozzie Smith goes after my first pitch, a fastball in on the hands, and bounces easily to third for the first out. Left-handed Steve Braun comes up to bat for Jim Kaat. A longtime American Leaguer and a favorite spot player of Cardinal manager Whitey Herzog, Braun had been doing well for the Cardinals. He had homered off Dick Ruthven for the only run in their 4–1 loss. In batting practice, Braun seemed to like the inside pitches most, but I saw that he could occasionally hit to the opposite alley.

I decide to set him up for a low, inside slider with fastballs. The strategy works somewhat in that he takes the slider for a strike to make the count 1–2, but when I try to finish him off with a fastball jammed in on the hands, he gets enough of the bat on the ball to trickle a single through the first-base hole into right field. The tying run will be coming up again in the person of leadoff hitter Tommy Herr.

I make sure to think positive thoughts as I rub up the baseball. "Give Braun credit for hitting the fastball and laying off the slider that he knew he couldn't hit," I tell myself. "Don't worry about the possible extra-base hits that Herr and Oberkfell might get to tie the game and knock you out." Instead, I remind myself that the top two hitters in the order have been hitless so far tonight, and I make up my mind to keep it that way.

I quickly get ahead of Herr with fastballs that he cannot get around on. The second one is a sinker, so I feel he is perfectly set up for the backdoor slider. It works like a charm. It starts off like a sinker off the outside corner, Tommy freezes at the plate, and the pitch breaks over the outside corner for a called third strike. Two out.

Kenny Oberkfell sees nothing but fastballs for the fourth time in a row. He had flied to center three straight times, but this time I keep him from hitting it even that far. He pops to short to end the top of the seventh inning.

As the fans rise for the seventh-inning stretch, I go down to the clubhouse to change undershirts for the fourth and last time of the game. I have held the two-run lead for six straight outs. There is no earthly reason why I cannot hold it for six more.

It is still 6–4 as I face Andy Van Slyke to begin the eighth inning. I note that I have helped myself tremendously in this game by getting the first two batters in the lineup—Herr and Oberkfell—so that I never have had to face the dangerous rookie with men on base. Van Slyke had homered off a slider, so I decide to go after him with my strength, a fastball on the outside part of the plate. It tails away from him. While he connects with some authority, he doesn't get it all. Darryl Strawberry makes a routine play of it in medium-deep right field for the first out.

George Hendrick comes up, and I immediately fall behind 2–0. The rising fastball comes too far inside and the slider misses low and away. There is no way that I am going to walk the tying run to the plate, so I go back to the basics: fastballs for low strikes. I move them in and out on George to even the count at 2–2. I detect that George is leaning toward the outside corner, so I surprise him with a low and in sinker that becomes a called third strike. Only my fourth strikeout of the night, but what a big one!

Tough Darrell Porter comes up now. While he had walked and scored in the three-run fourth, Darrell has not had the ball out of the infield against me tonight. I can see his determination to keep the inning alive. I am equally determined to end it so I can rest up for the ninth.

I decide to go right at him using fastballs with slight variations in speed and location. He swings at all three, gets a piece of the last two, so we're at 0–2 and holding. I expect a long at-bat now. While I continue to work quickly to keep my rhythm and my infielders alert, I consider ways of outguessing Darrell.

I know that he has fine power to all fields but that he is

basically a pull hitter looking for an inside pitch to drive. I try to keep him from pulling by throwing fastballs outside, but he fouls off the first one and takes the second one for ball one. My hoped-for strikeout slider, low and in, becomes ball two. He then fouls off two straight sliders, staying alive, and then takes a third slider high and in for ball three.

I have now lost the edge. From being in the driver's seat, 0–2, I now am one pitch away from bringing the tying run to the plate in the person of Willie McGee, who has broken out of his slump with two straight hits. On the positive side, after the three straight sliders, I feel that Darrell is set up for a running outside fastball. I fire the fastball and Darrell cannot pull it. He lofts a routine fly to our left fielder, George Foster, who gathers it in for the third out of the eighth inning.

I've thrown 120 pitches, but I've just retired the Cardinals 1–2–3 for the first time since the early innings. I confidently return to the bench and hope that the end of the game will be as smooth as the beginning. I vow to myself, "Stay away from 2–0 and 3–1 counts!" I had pitched with too many of them tonight (seven to be exact), and I know that you cannot expect to finish a game in the ninth inning if you are flirting with the danger of grooving pitches while behind in the count.

I start the ninth still protecting the two-run lead. I go after Willie McGee with fastballs, resolving that he will have to beat me with my best. On a 1–1 count, he hits a little grounder to Hernandez for out number one, unassisted. I steel myself for another difficult tussle with David Green. Sticking to the fastball at slightly different speeds and varying locations, I go to 1–1 on David.

Then comes a play that shows why we always talk in baseball about the importance of pitching *and* defense. David connects on a fastball that he drives up the middle. Jose Oquendo knocks the ball down with a great diving effort, but he cannot control it. It trickles into short center field and David hustles toward second base. Jose makes a great recovery, retrieves the ball, and fires a strike to Brian Giles covering second. Brian tags out the sliding Green. I've allowed a hit, but on the same play, my team has registered an out. The tying run won't be coming to the plate. What a wonderful feeling for a pitcher in this unpredictable game of baseball!

I am one out away from my goal, a complete game victory.

Jamie Quirk, a left-handed hitting utility player and another recent arrival from the American League, has his foot in the door as he comes up to pinch-hit for Ozzie Smith. I am glad that Dane Iorg, who is a dangerous, experienced National Leaguer, is unable to bat because of an injury, but Quirk has been swinging the bat well lately himself. He had doubled in two runs in the second game of the Monday night doubleheader. While not a home-run threat, Jamie can sting you in the alleys.

Within sight of my goal, I inexplicably lose my vision of the strike zone. I pull a "Van Slyke" and walk Quirk on four straight fastballs! Despite Jose's great play on David Green, the potential tying run will be coming up, after all.

Floyd Rayford, a right-handed hitter, is announced as the pinchhitter for pitcher John Martin. I gather my thoughts on the mound. I forget about the frustrating walk to Quirk, and concentrate on the positive. "I'm glad it's Rayford and not the leftie Iorg," I tell myself. "Go after him with fastballs and get him with the slider."

I proceed to do my job. Floyd takes a fastball tailing into him for strike one, and a sinker at the knees for strike two. He lays off a high, outside fastball for ball one, and then stays alive by getting a piece of a running fastball that I jam him with. Now I go for the kill.

I begin my stretch and glance over my shoulder at Jamie Quirk, who has a short lead at first. He is going nowhere with the tying run at the plate. I bring my right hand out of my glove quickly and up into throwing position in rhythm with my knee lift. For the 135th time tonight, I "get it out and get it up." I raise my arm to the forty-five degree angle to establish the downward plane toward home plate. The slider is released with the sharp twisting downward of my wrist. It feels good.

Rayford is off-balance and hits only a little part of the top of the ball. It rolls to Brian Giles at his normal second-base position. Brian scoops it up and tosses it easily to Keith Hernandez for the game-ending out. I have finished what I started out to do. One hundred thirty-five pitches may be a little more than I would like to have thrown, but I had done whatever was necessary to complete the job.

In years ahead, I may not look back at this game with any special memory, but as an illustration of the art of pitching, I think it serves a very useful purpose. There will always be rough spots in a baseball game. Even if you retire eleven in a row at the outset, as I did this time, don't be surprised if there is difficulty ahead. This is not to say that a pitcher must be mentally prepared to expect the other shoe to drop. No, that would make you defensive and a poorer pitcher.

What I mean to say is that the artful pitcher must take the inevitable peaks and valleys of pitching in stride and never give in to the batters or lose sight of his own strengths. On this day against the Cardinals. I made some bad pitches and suffered some lapses of control, but most important, my teammates had given me a lead and I had protected it.

I hope that this specific example of the art of pitching has helped to place the general points that I have made throughout this book in a clearer context. Like all arts, pitching has its occasional blemishes but always its consoling beauties. "Character" may be an overused word in sports, but Sandy Koufax once stated beautifully the importance of character for a pitcher: "Character means finding the grain of your craft and never wavering from it."

I hope youngsters who have the basic raw ability will be moved by this book to work at fulfilling their pitching potential. Pitching is a highly demanding profession, but I believe that harnessing your full mental and physical energies to become a successful pitcher will provide you with some of the happiest feelings that an athlete can ever experience.

BIBLIOGRAPHY

BOOKS

Alston, Walter, and Don Weiskopf. *The Complete Baseball Handbook: Strategies and Techniques for Winning*. Boston: Allyn and Bacon, 1972.

Jenkins, Ferguson, with Dave Fisher. *Inside Pitching*. Chicago: Henry Regnery, 1972.

Jenkins, Ferguson, with George Vass. *Like Nobody Else: The Fergie Jenkins Story*. Chicago: Henry Regnery, 1973.

Koufax, Sandy, with Ed Linn. *Koufax*. New York: Viking, 1966.

Kulund, Daniel N. *The Injured Athlete*. Philadelphia: Lippincott, 1982.

Marichal, Juan, with Charles Einstein. *A Pitcher's Story*. New York: Doubleday, 1967.

Mirkin, Gabe, and Marshall Hoffman. *The Sports Medicine Book*. Boston: Little, Brown and Company, 1978.

Official Baseball Rules, 1983 edition. (Published by *The Sporting News*.)

Palmer, Jim. *Pitching*, ed. Joel Cohen. New York: Atheneum, 1975.

Richards, Paul. *Modern Baseball Strategy*. New York: Prentice-Hall, 1955.

Ryan, Nolan, and Joe Torre, with Joel H. Cohen. *Pitching and Hitting*. Englewood Cliffs, N.J.: Prentice Hall, 1977.

Seaver, Tom. *Inside Corner: Talks with Tom Seaver*, ed. Joel H. Cohen. New York: Atheneum, 1974.

Seaver, Tom, with Steve Jacobson. *Pitching with Tom Seaver*. Englewood Cliffs, N.J.: Prentice Hall, 1973.

Shaw, Bob. *Pitching*. Chicago: Contemporary Books, 1972.

Sprague, Ken. *The Athlete's Body*. Boston: Houghton Mufflin–J.P. Tarcher, 1981.

Williams, Ted, and John Underwood. *The Science of Hitting*. New York: Simon and Schuster, 1971.

ARTICLES

Allman, William F. "Pitching Rainbows," *Science 82*, October 1982.

Drury, Joseph F., Jr. "The Hell It Don't Curve," reprinted in Einstein, Charles, ed. *The Baseball Reader*. New York: Lippincott and Crowell, 1982.

Jobe, Frank W., M.D., et al. "An EMG analysis of the shoulder in throwing and pitching: A preliminary report," *American Journal of Sports Medicine*, Vol. 11, No. 1 (1983).

Jobe, Frank W., M.D., and Diane Radovich Moynes, R. P. T., M.S. "Delineation of diagnostic criteria and a rehabilitation program for rotator cuff infuries," *American Journal of Sports Medicine*, Vol. 10, No. 6 (1982).

Ketejian, Armen. "To save his arm a pitcher should use head and study mechanics," *Sports Illustrated*, October 10, 1983.

Nirschl, Robert P., M.D. "Throwing or Swinging, the Shoulder Pays," *The Physician and Sports Medicine*, December 1974.

INDEX

H

Haddix, Harvey, 75, 76, 81
Hall of Fame, 14, 59, 116, 120
hamstring muscles, 44
Hands, Bill, 15
hands, breaking of, in pitch-
     ing motion, 75
heart rate, 38
heat prostration, 52
heel landing, in pitching
     motion, 85
Hendrick, George, 194–195,
     198–199, 204, 206
Hernandez, Keith, 129, 191,
     194, 195, 201, 203, 204,
     207, 208
Herr, Tommy, 197, 200–201,
     203, 205–206
Herzog, Whitey, 195, 203, 205
hesitancy, confidence vs., 20
hip movement, in pitching
     motion, 80
Hodges, Gil, 198
Hoefling, Gus, 37
home plate:
     backed up by pitcher, 155
     steal of, 160
hot weather, pitching in,
     13–14, 52
Houston, Astros, 121
Howard, Frank, 202
Hume, Tom, 21, 60–61
hurdler stretches, 47, 48

I

ice, therapeutic use of, 167
index finger, kept outside
     glove, 73–74
indicator signs, 163
infielders, throwing to,
     148–149

infraspinatus muscle, 24
     exercises for, 169
injuries:
     stiff front leg as cause of,
          60–61
     to upper body, 60
innings, first out of, 17
inside pitches, for batter
          claiming all of plate,
          17–18
internal rotators, 187
     exercises for, 34, 169, 171
Iorg, Dane, 194, 208
isokinetic exercises, 169,
          187–188
isometric exercises, 169,
          187–188
     internal-external, 173–175
     for supraspinatus muscle,
          184–185

J

Jackson, Reggie, 194
Japan, baseball in, 21, 158
Jenkins, Ferguson, 27, 37,
          39, 52, 56, 74, 163
     change-up of, 133, 137
     rising fastball of, 99, 104
     slider of, 128
John, Tommy, 39, 95, 131
Johnson, Walter, 94

K

Kaat, Jim, 203, 205
Kemp, Steve, 22
key outs, 15–16
Kiner, Ralph, 120
knee lift:
     pick-off motion and, 158
     in pitching motion, 77
knuckleball, 132, 141